Maya Angelou

Marcia Ann Gillespie,

Rosa Johnson Butler,

and Richard A. Long

Maya Angelou

A GLORIOUS CELEBRATION

Foreword by Oprah Winfrey

DOUBLEDAY

NEW YORK LONDON TORONTO

SYDNEY AUCKLAND

PUBLISHED BY DOUBLEDAY
a division of Random House, Inc.

Published in the United States by Doubleday, an imprint of The Doubleday Broadway
Publishing Group, a division of Random House, Inc., New York.
www.doubleday.com

DOUBLEDAY and the portrayal of an anchor with a dolphin are registered trademarks of
Random House, Inc.

LIBRARY OF CONGRESS CATALOGING-IN-PUBLICATION DATA
Gillespie, Marcia.
Maya Angelou : a glorious celebration / by Marcia Ann Gillespie, Rosa Johnson Butler,
and Richard A. Long.—1st ed.
p. cm.
1. Angelou, Maya.   I. Butler, Rosa Johnson.   II. Long, Richard A., 1927–   III. Title.
PS3551.N464Z67 2008
818'.5409—dc22
2007031301

ISBN 978-0-385-51108-7

PRINTED IN THE UNITED STATES OF AMERICA

1 3 5 7 9 10 8 6 4 2

FIRST EDITION

FROM MARCIA ANN GILLESPIE

For my late parents,
Ethel and Charles Gillespie,
who loved me up and urged me on.

FROM ROSA JOHNSON BUTLER

To God, I'm thankful for my life.

To Mother, I'm thankful to God for you and
your love for me.

To my loving Auntie Maya . . . Thank you for
always being in my corner and for telling me years
ago, "God loves you and wants the best for you."

FROM RICHARD A. LONG

For M. J. Hewitt

It is good to have an end to journey towards;
but it is the journey that matters in the end.

URSULA K. LeGUIN

Contents

I was still in shock ...
murder ... had demora...
There seemed to be no cent...
universe and the known
world had withdrawn
and inscrutable ...
I was further consumed
Guy in Africa ... wrapped
... became a hair shirt
which I could not dislod...
newly found and desperately
mannishness caused him to
something to irritate the ...
anxiety guilt terror and ...
I had brought to Louis a
few months ... pestilen...

Maya Angelou

POEMS

FOREWORD

*I*N ALL THE DAYS OF MY LIFE, I NEVER MET A woman who was more completely herself than Maya Angelou. She fully inhabits and owns every space of herself with no pretense and no false modesty. She has a certain way of being in this world. When you walk into a room and she's there, you know it. She is fully aware of what it means to be human, and share that humanity with others. Being around her makes you want to do the same, be more fully your own self.

She's been teaching me about being myself since I was a young girl and first read *I Know Why the Caged Bird Sings*. At the time (1969), I couldn't believe a young woman's story with so many similarities to my own had merited a book. Being raised in the South by a grandmother, learning to love poetry, raped at seven, growing up speaking in the church—all mirrored my own tenuous and tumultuous upbringing. Reading about her life gave value to my own. The fact that she had not merely survived but triumphed allowed me to see the possibility of my own victory over adversity.

And so the lessons began for me long before I met her. I see now the absolute divine order that brought us together. I was a young reporter in Baltimore having admired her from afar, memorizing, and then reciting her poetry to anyone who would listen. When she came to town I convinced my station manager that I had to be the one to interview her. This was a once-in-a-lifetime opportunity to meet the woman I most admired who'd been a mentor to me without even knowing it. I asked her for five minutes of her time to please speak to me on camera. I was careful not to take a second more than I'd asked for. At the end of the five minutes, she inquired with a quizzical smile, "Who are you, girl?"

That was the beginning of a lifelong sister-mother-daughter friendship. She has been for me a refuge and an anchor.

I've literally sat at her feet (in my pj's) listening, listening, listening to her revelations on the intricacies of life. I've felt touched by grace to share in her wisdom.

"When people show you who they are, believe them the first time." She taught me this treasure of a lesson and so many others that helped me to be a real woman and not just an "aging female" as she is fond to note.

From her I learned the first words to say when faced with any challenge or crisis: "Thank you." "Say 'thank you'," she says, because God always puts a rainbow in the clouds and abides on the side of what is true.

She taught me what she knows for sure and explained so eloquently in her poem "Grandmothers"—"When you learn teach, when you get give." And the lesson we all eventually must evolve to learn: "We are all more alike than we are different."

I marvel that this woman whom I grew up loving from a distance became such an intricate and powerful influence in my life. All of her friends and family feel as I do, blessed to know her.

It's only appropriate as she moves into her eightieth year that this book is written as an acknowledgment and affirmation of her favorite word, "joy," as we celebrate the joy she has shared with so many.

Her life is a teaching gift to us all.

—*Oprah Winfrey*

CHAPTER I

Truths Told

*I hope to look through my life at life. I want to use
what has happened to me—is happening to me—to
see what human beings are like.*

—MAYA ANGELOU (1992)

for a few month I was a novelty
then the attendance began to wane
I was told that people had gone
other place to listen to a real singer
riously led me. Then came a night
when there was a decided drop. Aftereffectiveness. Night after night attenda
began to wane until it became
common to find the club only a
ll at showtime I was told tha
rival had hired an aut
thentic singer. I went alone to t
to see my competitor and the
spat the show made me come to
terms with my life.

Della Reese was announced au
when she appeared there was an
audible gasp. She was nearly six feet
ll and very beautiful and wat
wearing what could be called a pro
gown. There were no sequins or bea
or shiny stars on her dress. She was
certainly not in costume sta

$\mathcal{S}$HE'S THE TALL, IMPOSING COCOA-SKINNED WOMAN standing in the winter's chill, the poet reminding the nation and its leaders of the fragility of our planet, the wonder of life, the hope of humankind at William Jefferson Clinton's first inauguration as President of the United States. She's the writer sharing hard-earned wisdom, humorous and painful truths and powerful affirmations, urging her readers to laugh, to dare, to strive, to dream, to love, to say Yes! to life. The autobiographer whose frank thoughtful sharing of her life's journey continues to captivate, challenge, and inspire

Maya Angelou delivering her poem "On the Pulse of Morning" at William Jefferson Clinton's inauguration as president of the United States of America in 1993. *(Courtesy of the White House)*

readers of all ages around the world. The much sought after speaker urging her audiences to own their truths, claim their voices, and fully embrace their lives. Calling us to higher ground, her words nurture our spirits, stretch our minds, and stir our hearts. Her messages affirm our shared humanity, the human experience, and the sacredness of life. We laugh and rejoice with her. She challenges us and calls us to love ourselves and one another, to live fully, savor life, and embrace our potential. Her voice—hot chocolate smooth, melodious and welcoming—holds listeners spellbound. Her laughter starts deep, envelopes, and invites us all to share the joy.

Her name is Maya Angelou.

And hers is a rich life. She's danced and sung in theaters and nightclubs, acted, written, and directed works for the stage, television, and film. She's a college professor, serious scholar, and a generous mentor. She's the loving mother of one son, a proud grandmother, and wise, doting great-grandmother. She's a woman with a grand passion for life that she's shared with husbands and soulmates, with family, chosen kin, and an enduring ever-expanding circle of friends; she lives the life she sings about on the page to the fullest. Her homes, elegantly appointed, always welcoming and comfortable, abound with hundreds of books and the art that she's collected all of her adult life. Her skill in the kitchen is the stuff of legend—from haute cuisine to down-home comfort food—and the source of great pleasure for both the cook and those invited to share. At her table God is always thanked, food savored, laughter and rich talk encouraged. She revels in gathering folk around her, in her home, at her table, ever welcoming.

Now, as she steps into the eightieth year of her life, she remains as curious and zestful as a young woman, maintaining a schedule that many people half her age would find daunting. She spends weeks traveling the blue highways of America in her customized bus en route to speaking engagements before audiences ranging from children and college students to folks from all walks of life. Wherever she goes there are always interviews to be given; television and radio appearances; book signings; meetings with local officials, community groups, activists, writers and artists, but she always finds time to share laughter and break bread with friends old and new.

Ever the writer, disciplined and focused, whether on the road or at home, she works at her craft. She writes in longhand on yellow legal pads, poetry and prose in constant progress. She is the creator of a very successful, special collection of products for Hallmark that ranges from greeting cards to decorative accessories in the sumptuous fabrics and jewel colors that she loves. Her passion for theater and film is undiminished. There are always directing, acting, writing projects in the mix or on her to-do list. And then there's her work as a distinguished professor at Wake Forest University in Winston-Salem, North Carolina, where she holds a lifetime chair and students vie for admission to her seminar series.

The woman who never attended college has been the recipient of dozens of honorary degrees in recognition of all her accomplishments and takes due pride in being called Dr. Angelou. A serious scholar and formidable intellectual thinker, she's ever curious, open to learning, to new ideas, to questions. She's a voracious and eclectic reader and a connoisseur of libraries. She is multilingual, fluent in French, Spanish, Fanti, Italian, and Arabic—a reflection of a native gift, a highly tuned ear and appreciation for the nuances of language, and of her keen desire to live in the world.

Living in the world also means working to improve the quality of life on the planet. She is and has long been a tireless activist lending support to efforts to improve the lives of women and children, championing education, racial, gender, social, and economic justice, human rights, and peace.

She's a woman, an African American woman, a Renaissance woman in the truest sense of the word.

Her name is Maya Angelou.

When at home in her primary residence in Winston-Salem, Maya Angelou often sits at a table strategically placed in a nook midway between her open kitchen and formal dining and living rooms. The many cookbooks that she's collected throughout the years are on shelves in easy reach. From her seat at the table Maya can easily turn to check on the activity in her kitchen, reminding her housekeeper to stir a pot or instructing her on how to season a dish. It's where she reads correspondence, handles many of her business affairs, often chats with friends and family and shares in formal meals. She always keeps a deck of cards close for the many games of solitaire—played to occupy her "Little Mind" and free up her "big mind." There are always books around—her own and those of others—to be read or signed, shared or referenced, and yellow legal pads, personalized stationery, and pens close at hand. Among the books there are three well-thumbed constants: a thesaurus, a dictionary, and a Bible. A beautifully wrought ceramic angel with a beaming smile, a gift from her son Guy, stands sentinel.

Her table sits close to a multi-windowed wall offering a clear view of the many tall trees, the natural and carefully landscaped beauty of her grounds. At the base of the window photographs of her biological and chosen family cluster, smiling faces and group shots, in varying life stages. But her chair faces the nook's narrow, rouge-red wall, a space she has reserved to honor and remember three of her ancestors. Their photographs quietly dominate the space. To the left there is her paternal grandmother, Annie Hender-

Dr. Maya Angelou! She has delivered commencement speeches and received honorary degrees from dozens of universities and colleges in the United States and abroad. Shown on this page at Northeastern University *(courtesy Northeastern University Library, Archives and Special Collections Department)* and Brown University, 1984 *(courtesy Brown University)*; on the opposite page at Boston College *(courtesy John J. Burns Library, Boston College)*, Rollins College, 1985 *(courtesy Department of College Archives and Special Collections, Olin Library, Rollins College)*, Durham University in the U.K., 1995 *(by permission of Durham University)*

Annie Henderson, Maya's paternal grandmother, was a towering presence in her granddaughter's life (photo circa 1930s). *(Angelou-Johnson Family Archives)*

son, a study in serenity; to the right her mother, Vivian Baxter, her vivacious spirit shining through; and below, the solemn, unflinching gaze of her paternal great-grandmother, Kentucky Shannon: three women, all iron-willed, powerful spirits, who in their time dared to stand their ground and claim their lives. Maya Angelou never forgets the people who gave her life, the bloodline she shares, the spiritual legacy she carries.

Her great-grandmother had been born into slavery. When freedom came she claimed her independence by choosing to rename herself Kentucky Shannon. Generations later her great-granddaughter would choose to rename herself when setting her face to the future. When she was born in St. Louis, Missouri, on April 4, 1928, her parents, Bailey Johnson and Vivian Baxter Johnson, named her Marguerite. She was their second child. A son, whom they named Bailey after his father, had been born a year earlier.

Her father, Bailey Johnson, was a son of the rural South, one among the legions of Black migrants drawn north to escape the South's blatant, violent oppression and in search of a better life. Her mother, born and raised in St. Louis, was every inch an urban woman. She, one of two daughters surrounded by four brothers, was smart and sassy, sophisticated and daring. Nothing and no one ever seemed to intimidate her. Vivian Baxter was a woman ahead of her time. Her father was the younger of two sons. He was big and handsome and also a bit of a cynic, whose mannered speech and personal style reflected his desire to distance himself from his rural southern roots. Vivian and Bailey's daughter would inherit her parents' magnetic personalities, their powerful egos, and their strong independent streaks.

When Marguerite was still a babe in arms the young family packed their bags and headed west. Her parents must have dazzled each other when they met and married in St. Louis, but their tumultuous union imploded in California. Perhaps the qualities that drew them to each other also tore them apart. After the marriage collapsed, the three-year-old Marguerite and her brother, Bailey, were sent to Stamps, Arkansas, to live with their paternal grandmother.

Maya's paternal great-grandmother declared her personal independence when slavery was abolished by taking the name Kentucky Shannon. This photo is one of a grouping of Maya's female ancestors that hangs in constant view on the wall facing her as she sits at her favorite work table in her home in North Carolina. (*Angelou-Johnson Family Archives*)

They put me and my brother on a train, without any companionship, without any adult, put tags on our arms, and said, "This child should be delivered to Miss Annie Henderson in Stamps, Ark." . . .

For years I thought what they'd done was a terrible thing, but then I found out that Bailey and I were just part of a legion of black children whose parents had taken them out of the South thinking that things would be better for them. Unfortunately that wasn't always so, and the parents would send the children back south to their grandparents, while the parents scuffled and sweated trying to make a better life . . .

—AS TOLD TO MARCIA ANN GILLESPIE

(LEFT) William James Johnson, Maya's paternal grandfather, was a minister. *(Angelou-Johnson Family Archives)*

(CENTER) Maya may have inherited her multilingual skill from her father, Bailey James Johnson. He became fluent in French while serving in World War I and picked up Spanish when he moved to California. *(Angelou-Johnson Family Archives)*

(BELOW) Maya's mother, Vivian Baxter, also known as Lady B, shown here on horseback in California in the 1940s, had an adventurous, independent spirit, a quick wit, and an enormous zest for life. *(Angelou-Johnson Family Archives)*

Stamps was a small rural community, two communities really, one Black the other White, warily coinciding under the toxic strictures of segregation. The Black folks in Stamps were tight-knit; they all knew each other. They shared memories, history, and often blood. They had few worldly possessions and struggled to make do, but they were sustained by a thriving folk culture, a rich spiritual life, and a powerful, finely tuned sense of community.

Annie Henderson was an extraordinary woman. She married three times, bore two sons and single-handedly built her own business. She was a woman of substance and stature in her community, a pillar of her church, humble in her faith, and a great judge of human nature. It was in her paternal grandmother's keeping that the little Marguerite Johnson found safe harbor. So much of her wisdom and grace, her sensibilities and faith stem from this source.

Maya's paternal grandmother, Annie Henderson, was one of five sisters. She is shown here (right) with her favorite sister, Maya's Aunt Ida, and a neighbor's child. (*Angelou-Johnson Family Archives*)

One of my earliest memories of Mamma, of my grandmother, is a glimpse of a tall cinnamon-colored woman with a deep, soft voice, standing thousands of feet up in the air on nothing visible. That incredible vision was the result of what my imagination would do each time Mamma drew herself up to her full six feet, clasped her hands be-

hind her back, looked up into the distant sky, and said "I will step out on the word of God."

—MAYA ANGELOU, *WOULDN'T TAKE NOTHING FOR MY JOURNEY NOW*, RANDOM HOUSE, 1993

Annie Henderson was the proprietor of the only general store in the Black community, no mean feat for a woman, especially a barely literate Black woman in that place and time. That store was the result of years of hard labor cooking and selling food to the cotton and sawmill workers, and a shrewd business instinct. She lived and worked there with her other son, the children's Uncle Willie, who as a child had been badly crippled in an accident. The store was a focal point for the Black community and a never-ending source of wonder for Maya and her brother.

It was a glorious place. I remember the wonderful smells; the aroma of the pickle barrel, the bulging sacks of corn, the luscious, ripe fruit. You could pick up a can of snuff from North Carolina, a box of matches from Ohio, a yard of ribbon from New York. All of those places seemed terribly exotic to me. I would fantasize how people from there had actually touched those objects. It was a magnificent experience!

—STEPHANIE STOKES OLIVER, "MAYA ANGELOU: THE HEART OF THE WOMAN," *ESSENCE*, MAY 1983

Maya's paternal uncle Willie Johnson (right, shown here in the 1940s with an unidentified friend), who lived and worked in the family store in Stamps, played a significant role in Maya's upbringing. *(Angelou-Johnson Family Archives)*

Annie Henderson was a woman with a deep faith, unflinching honesty, profound wisdom and an abiding love for her family, which informed the life lessons she sought to teach her grandchildren: "At least ten times a year my grandmother would tell me . . . "Sister, if you see something you don't like, do everything you can do, that's right to do, to change it. And if you can't change it, change the way you think about it." Over the years, I learned how absolutely right she was." (Jann Malone, "The Passions of Maya Angelou," *Times-Dispatch,* March 25, 2007)

In Stamps, Marguerite Johnson developed her love of nature, absorbed the folk wisdom and culture whose roots stretched back to West Africa, embraced faith in the bosom of the Black church, and witnessed the power of the word—spoken and sung—and of music to move people to higher ground. And it was in the church that she, like so many Black children, was encouraged to stand and speak in front of the public reciting poetry or selected prose in special programs. She was a thoughtful, studious seven-year-old—taller than her age mates—when her big, talkative, "blindingly handsome" father swooped back into his children's lives. He had come to take them to St. Louis to live with their mother. For her brother, Bailey, the move to the big city was an adventure. Bailey was totally enraptured by

Annie Henderson's grocery store where the family lived and worked in Stamps, Arkansas. It had been abandoned by the time this snapshot was taken in the 1970s. A complete replica of the store is on display at the Museum of Tolerance in Los Angeles, California. *(Angelou-Johnson Family Archives)*

Marguerite Johnson (Maya Angelou) at the age of eight, not long after being returned to her grandmother Annie Henderson in Stamps, Arkansas. *(Angelou-Johnson Family Archives)*

his mother and overjoyed to be with her again. Reconnecting with the mother she barely knew and her worldly wise maternal kin, adapting to a fast urban pace, a new school, and making new friends was a more challenging adjustment for Marguerite.

Grandmother Henderson had been her rock, a solid predictable presence. Her mother, though diminutive in size, was a powerful force, strong and decisive, a bold risk taker, with an effervescent and far more volatile personality. "To describe my mother would be to write about a hurricane in its perfect power. Or the climbing, falling colors of a rainbow." (Maya Angelou, *I Know Why the Caged Bird Sings,* Random House, 1970).

When Vivian Baxter was in a room one paid attention. But she was not the mother the little girl from Stamps had longed for:

My mother has had a more profound influence on me since I've been an adult than she did as a child. I've come to the conclusion that some adults are not really qualified to be parents of young children. They make much better parents of adults. My mother is that type.

Today, we have a much closer relationship. She knows how to be a friend, and when to stay out of my business. However, I felt very little positive influence from her as a child. I owe much more to my grandmother and my brother, whom I credit with saving my life—both my mental and spiritual life, as well as my breathing-in and breathing-out life.

—JEFFREY ELLIOTT, "MAYA ANGELOU RAPS," *SEPIA,* OCTOBER 1977

In St. Louis, Marguerite got to know her maternal kin: the Baxter's were a fierce clan. Her maternal grandmother was a politically savvy wheeler-dealer who wielded a great deal of power in the Black community. Her hardworking maternal grandfather doted on his wife and children and encouraged their independence. And people minded their p's and q's around Vivian and her siblings, who were all hot-tempered and dangerous when riled.

Marguerite's life's journey might well have been markedly different if she'd remained with her maternal kin. But little more than a year after being reunited with her mother the shy little girl was sexually violated by one of her mother's male friends, and further traumatized by having to testify at her victimizer's trial. After the trial, the man was attacked and killed by unknown assailants, some said by the Baxters, and the wounded little girl simply shut down.

After my mother's lover raped me when I was seven, I didn't speak for six years. Because I gave the man's name to my brother and he'd given it to the family, I thought my voice had killed him. So I just held it. I did talk to my brother now and again. Because I loved him so much I knew my voice couldn't hurt him. Fifty years later, about a year before he died, I mentioned that to him. He burst out laughing and said that most of the time he couldn't understand a word I was saying.

—AS TOLD TO MARCIA ANN GILLESPIE

When all of her efforts to get her daughter to speak failed, Vivian reluctantly agreed to send Marguerite and Bailey back to their grandmother Annie. The two children who returned to Stamps were markedly changed. Bailey, who had embraced city life and adored his mother, grew ever more restless and frustrated in the country. But Marguerite was a wounded bird in need of healing. In Stamps, her grandmother accepted her muteness with the sure belief that one day the child would reclaim her voice. And Bailey became her champion; speaking for her when needed, protecting her right to silence. It was during this period that Marguerite's extraordinary memory—her ability to retain vast amounts of information, her retention of favorite poems and passages from the many books she devoured—kicked into high gear. And in her silence she became—and remains—an intense listener and observer, attuned to words spoken and things unsaid.

Encouraged by her first adult friend and mentor, Mrs. Bertha Flowers, a cultured, educated Black woman who was a rare bird in Stamps, Marguerite reclaimed her voice and her enduring love for the written word took firm hold. In books of poetry and prose she discovered a world of possibilities and the rich, complex, ever unfolding tapestry of the human experience.

I was Danton and Madame Defarge and all those people in *A Tale of Two Cities*. I was Daphne du Maurier and the Brontë sisters in a town where blacks were not allowed to cross the street. I was educated by those writers. Not about themselves and their people, but about me, what I could hope for.

—LAURENCE TOPPMAN, "MAYA ANGELOU: THE SERENE SPIRIT OF A SURVIVOR," *CHARLOTTE OBSERVER*, DECEMBER 11, 1983

Speaking of the impact of her reading upon her ultimate vocation she has said,

> There were two men who probably formed my writing ambition more than any others. They were Paul Laurence Dunbar and William Shakespeare. I love them. I love the rhythm and sweetness of Dunbar's dialect verse. I love "Candle Lighting Time" and "Little Brown Baby." I also love James Weldon Johnson's "Creation."
> —CLAUDIA TATE, ED., *BLACK WOMEN WRITERS AT WORK*, CONTINUUM, 1983

Not only did Marguerite Johnson reclaim her voice, she recaptured her joy, her curiosity, and her spirit. But although Stamps had been

a safe haven for the Johnson grandchildren when they were young, and a healing ground for the traumatized girl, it had little to offer two intelligent, spirited black teenagers. And for Bailey in particular, with his bodacious personality, quick tongue, and sensitive spirit there was much to fear in a land known for its chain gangs and lynchings. In 1942, when Marguerite

Marguerite Johnson (Maya) at fifteen, shortly after she arrived in San Diego, California, to spend the summer of 1943 with her father. (Angelou-Johnson Family Archives)

was fourteen, her grandmother announced that she and her brother were going to live with their mother in California. It was time.

Stamps, Arkansas, had been her Gilead, her grandmother's wisdom and love her balm. California would become her crucible, challenging her spirit and igniting a passion for the arts. Her mother's energy and tough love would fuel her daughter's desire for self-reliance. After Vivian's father died the entire Baxter family moved to California. They were living in Oakland when Marguerite and Bailey came to join their mother. Vivian, though trained as a nurse, had become a professional card player and supported herself and her children from her winnings. But not long after being reunited with her children, she married a relatively prosperous self-made businessman who moved them into his big house in San Francisco, which they shared with a number of tenants.

The six-foot-tall Marguerite may have stood head and shoulders above her mother, but Vivian Baxter was a towering presence in her daughter's life. A magnetic personality, she was eager and open to adventure, to different people, cultures, food, and to life. Wherever Vivian lived she gathered people around her, there

Marguerite Johnson (Maya) at fifteen. *(Angelou-Johnson Family Archives)*

was always laughter, good food and flowing drinks, card games, tall tales and true talk. She believed in living well, loved beautiful things, took pride in her appearance and her living space. But Vivian Baxter was not a woman to be messed with. She carried a switchblade and packed a pistol and had used them on more than one occasion.

Single-minded when in pursuit of a goal, she was a tough judge of human nature. She believed people should own their lives, be accountable for their actions. She shared her zest for life and her unflinching sense of personal accountability and independence with her daughter, a daughter who often longed for a more nurturing presence.

At about 22 . . . for some incredible reason, I saw my
mother separate from me. Absolutely separate. And I
thought, I see, you're not really my mother, the mother
I wanted and needed; you're a character. And I began to
see her like a character I would have read about. Now that
didn't mean that in lonely or bitter or painful moments I
didn't still want her to be that big-bosomed, open-armed,
steady, consistent person. But I'd say that 60 percent of
the time I saw her as a character. Then it grew to be 70
percent. Then 80. And then my own resistance allowed
me to accept her as the character.

—MARY CHAMBERLAIN, ED., "ROSA GUY AND MAYA ANGELOU,"
IN *WRITING LIVES: CONVERSATIONS BETWEEN WOMEN WRITERS*,
VIRAGO, 1988

The relationship between mother and daughter ripened over time. As adults they became friends, women who truly enjoyed each other's company. And Vivian, known affectionately as Lady B and lovingly called BB by her daughter, became more the mother that her daughter had longed for when she was a girl and still needed as an adult, always there to provide succoring mother love when needed.

If her mother was like a perfect storm, her father, Bailey Johnson, was a study in contradictions and a far more distant presence in his daughter's life. Her father had settled in San Diego, California. An excellent cook who worked in the kitchen at the local Naval Hospital, he described himself as a naval dietitian. And he took great pride in being an upstanding member of two fraternal organizations, the Masons and the Elks, and the first Black man to be named a deacon in his Lutheran Church.

As a child Marguerite had found his mannered, affected speech and need to be the center of attention off-putting. The teenaged Marguerite, in the course of a near disastrous summer sojourn with him, came to a far more mature understanding of the man.

It seemed hard to believe that he was a lonely person, searching relentlessly in bottles, under women's skirts, in church work and lofty job titles for his "personal niche," lost before birth and unrecovered since. It was obvious to me that he had never belonged in Stamps. . . . How maddening it was to have been born in a cotton field with aspirations of grandeur.

—ANGELOU, *I KNOW WHY THE CAGED BIRD SINGS*

While living with her father she'd accompanied him on a quick trip to Mexico where he'd gotten drunk and passed out in a local cantina. Determined to get them safely back across the border that night she took the wheel of his car and taught herself to drive on a dusty Mexican road. During that fateful summer of 1943, she would also learn that her father was often more concerned about the appearance of things rather than their substance. He chose to be amused and later to ignore the increasing hostility between his fifteen-year-old daughter and the woman he was living with. And when that relationship ended in an explosion of violence that left Marguerite stabbed and bleeding, he failed to stand up for his daughter. Choosing to remain with his girlfriend, he left Marguerite first in the care of others and then alone to recuperate in an empty house. Still healing, unwilling to inform her mother about the stabbing for fear that her hot-tempered Baxter kin would retaliate, Marguerite chose to walk away. Though it had almost cost her her life, she'd refused to be cowed by her father's girlfriend. And in keeping with her grandmother's teaching not to complain and her mother's firm belief in personal accountability, Marguerite had chosen to stand and survive on her own.

She spent weeks living on the streets in San Diego, sleeping in abandoned cars, joining forces with other homeless young people who befriended her. She waited until she'd fully recovered from her injuries before calling her mother and arranging to return home.

During the course of that tumultuous summer the teenaged Marguerite Johnson took ownership of her life. Once back in her mother's home she was like a fish out of water, more mature than her age mates in so many ways. The Second World War was still raging, intensifying and speeding the pulse of life. Determined to test her wings, instead of going right back to high school for the fall term, Marguerite convinced her mother that she was ready to go to work. She applied for a job as a conductor on the city's fabled trolleys. Undeterred by the fact that those jobs had been reserved for Whites she pushed the envelope and broke through the color line. She became the city's first "Negro" conductor. It was considered a plum job, but after missing the first semester her hunger for knowledge won out and she returned to high school.

Although she excelled in school, Marguerite was a restless student, frequently skipping classes to wander the city, often exploring museums and libraries. Her experiences made her seem far more mature than her classmates, but Marguerite Johnson was still a girl struggling to find and claim her womanhood. And like so many girls on the same quest, she focused on deconstructing the mystery of sex, love, and relationships as the key to woman country. She approached it like some "misguided scientist," selecting a handsome young man from the neighborhood, hoping that offering him sex would lead to something more. It did. But instead of a fairy-tale ending, her one encounter resulted in pregnancy. So there she was a high school senior, pregnant and hiding it from everyone, waiting until the eighth month, waiting until after her graduation day, to inform her family.

What becomes of an unwed teenaged mother in the 1940s? Shame and blame? A shotgun marriage? Dreams sidetracked? Low-wage work? It was 1945, the war was finally over, when Marguerite Johnson, at seventeen, became the mother of a baby boy who she named Clyde. She was luckier than many young women in similar situations. Her family stood by her. They never blamed her, never insisted upon marriage, but they made it clear that they expected her to be responsible for herself and her son. And she was equally determined to prove that she could, in fact, stand on her own.

Those early years of motherhood tested her mettle. She left home seeking work, forced to leave her baby in the care of others. She tried the fast life—as the front woman/business manager for prostitutes—and while working as a cook in a restaurant, lonely and living miles from her family, briefly got lured into prostitution herself. She sought haven in Stamps with her baby, but her refusal to bend to the rules of segregation killed any dreams she had about living there. Once back in San Francisco, she even tried to join the army, only to be turned down because she'd briefly taken dance and acting lessons at a union-backed school (the California Labor School) that had been labeled Communist.

She'd found pleasure but not true companionship or permanence in a number of relationships. And then while working in a record store in 1951 she met Enistasious (Tosh) Angelos. The son of Greek immigrants, the handsome former sailor worked in an electrical store, but dreamed of becoming a professional musician. He

Bailey James Johnson Jr., Maya's brother, was one year older than she and very much her protective big brother. *(Angelou-Johnson Family Archives)*

courted Marguerite, making it clear that he wanted to marry her and be a father to her son. But an interracial marriage in the 1950s was a giant step, illegal in many states and anathema in both communities. He was poor and White, and her mother disapproved of him on both counts. It was her brother, Bailey, who urged her to follow her heart.

One of the things that drew her to marry was her desire for security, more for her son than for herself. When her son was born she determined to set her own course on the sea of motherhood and politely declined most of the advice she received from others.

> I expected to be his teacher. So because of him I educated myself. When he was four, I started him reading because I loved to read and he would interrupt when I was reading. So I taught him to read. But then he'd ask questions and I would say, "I'm not prepared to answer that now, but later this evening when you come from school we'll talk about it." And off I'd go to the library. I've learned an awful lot because of him.
>
> —STOKES OLIVER, "MAYA ANGELOU: THE HEART
> OF THE WOMAN"

For a time the marriage seemed on solid ground. Tosh was a loving husband and had closely bonded with her six-year-old son, Clyde; he was the breadwinner and Marguerite was a full-time mother and housewife. But a marriage is a social contract, and this one lacked community support. And to her dismay, Marguerite discovered that her husband had a possessive and controlling nature.

(OPPOSITE) Maya and her son, Guy Johnson, sharing laughter while walking the beach in northern California in the late 1970s. *(Photo by Mary Ellen Mark)*

The strain took its toll, the couple had few friends, and Marguerite, in trying to achieve the happy home ideal touted in the women's magazines of the era, had forfeited too much of herself. Ironically, Tosh was the first to express dissatisfaction with the marriage. They had been together less than two years. It was her wake-up call. And in the end, it was she who walked away.

Maya dancing on the beach. *(Photo by Marlene Callahan Wallace)*

CHAPTER 2

Becoming an Artist

*You can become truly accomplished at something
you love.*

—MAYA ANGELOU (2000)

for a few month I was a novelty
then the attendance began to wane
I was told that people had gone
other close to listen to a real singer
riosity led me. Then came a nigh
ew there was a decided drop. Af
iveness. Night after night attenda
egan to wane until it became
mon to find the club only a
ll at showtime I was told tha
rival had hired an
thentic singer. I went alone to
to see my competition and the
spa show made me come to
grips with my life.

Della Reese was announced an
hen she appeared there was an
dible gasp. She was nearly six feet
ll and very beautiful and was
earing what could be called a pro
own. There were no sequins or bea
r phony stars on her dress. She was
tainly not

*I*N THE EARLY 1950S women were aggressively social-
ized to marry and become submissive helpmates. In deciding to end
her marriage, Marguerite Johnson Angelos recognized that she had
nearly allowed herself to succumb to that spirit-stifling notion of
the good wife.

> I thought it would be magnificent if I could be the June
> Allyson type—you know, have a big house, a station
> wagon, and lots of kids. I would stay home, of course,
> and do the cooking and the cleaning. My husband would
> have a good job and bring home the money. He would tell
> me what to think and how to act. I thought that would be
> heaven. I found it to be sheer hell!
>
> —JEFFREY M. ELLIOT, "MAYA ANGELOU RAPS"

Fortunately she had other, more powerful role models to draw
from: her paternal grandmother and her mother, women who each
in her own way chose to set her own course and to own her life. And
it was in keeping with their spirits and her own that Marguerite
Johnson Angelos determined to step out on faith and reach for her
dream.

She wanted to be a dancer!

It was a dream born in high school when, out of the blue, she'd received a scholarship to the California Labor School to study theater and dance. Although she'd never taken formal dance lessons before, at the Labor School Marguerite Johnson discovered that she had real talent as a dancer, and acting seemed like a natural extension of the many hours she had spent imagining herself as a character in one of her cherished books. But dancing was her first love.

Before her marriage, she'd had a brief stint as a professional dancer that ended when her dance partner reneged on an agreement. And whenever she could afford it she attended performances in San Francisco and took modern dance classes. At one of those classes she met two fellow dancers, Alvin Ailey and Ruth Beckford, who would become her lifelong friends. (Ailey and Beckford went on to make their marks in dance, he as one of the great dancer-choreographers, and she for dancing with and writing about the great Katherine Dunham.) Marguerite and Alvin formed a dance team, billing themselves as Al and Rita. The duo appeared at a number of local civic and fraternal functions in and around San Francisco: "Alvin wore a leopard print G-string and I wore a homemade costume of a few feathers and even fewer sequins. We danced to Duke Ellington's 'Caravan.' Alvin had choreographed the routine" (Angelou, *Wouldn't Take Nothing for My Journey Now*).

In his autobiography Ailey fondly recalled working with her: "For a month or so we rehearsed our routine, with both of us making up the steps. That was the first time I had ever attempted any kind of choreography. She was quite a stimulus. . . . Could do the most extraordinary moves. I spent more time watching her than I did doing choreography" (Alvin Ailey with A. Peter Bailey, *Revelations:*

The Autobiography of Alvin Ailey, Birch Lane Press/Carol Publishing Group, 1995). The dancing duo of Al and Rita never took flight. But years later Ailey's work with another tall, incredibly talented dancer named Judith Jamison would become the stuff of legend.

Shortly after she married Tosh Angelos in 1951 Marguerite applied for and won a scholarship to study with Pearl Primus, one of the trailblazers in making African dance part of the African American canon. With her new husband's blessing Marguerite and Clyde moved to New York and stayed with musician friends of Tosh's, who later joined them. They spent a year in the city—Marguerite studying with Primus, Tosh working on his music. She had high hopes that the scholarship might lead to something permanent, but opportunities for Black dancers were few and far between, and the competition was fierce. Although she'd taken classes whenever she could, she remembered "I had no chance to become a great dancer. I simply didn't have enough training." They moved back to San Francisco where Tosh could find steady work.

When her marriage ended in 1953, wanting to dance, needing to earn a living, Marguerite finally found a job dancing at the Garden of Allah, a strip joint in San Francisco's International section.

My costume consisted of two sequins and a feather . . .
I danced fifteen minutes of every hour, six times a night.
The other ladies would go out and strip, and the band
would play, "Tea for Two," or something like that, because
the women weren't into what they were doing, and the
band was bored with all that grind, grind, grind. But I was
a dancer and I loved it. Each time I danced they *played* for

me—all sorts of wonderful things like "Caravan." And we
had a fabulous time.

—STEPHANIE CARUANA, "MAYA ANGELOU: AN INTERVIEW,"
PLAYGIRL, OCTOBER 1974

As word spread about this lithe, six-foot-tall, brown-skinned
beauty who danced up a storm, a new set of customers began to
make their way to the Garden of Allah. Among them were a group
of musicians and performers who would change her life. One of
them, Jorie Amos, was singing at the Purple Onion, a cabaret
known as a showcase for rising stars. At a party one night Jorie com-
plained about being constantly asked to sing calypso songs. In re-
buttal Marguerite, who loved calypso music with its wise, witty, and
sly lyrics sang "Run Joe" and bowled them all over. Before the party
ended the group was conspiring to get her hired to replace Jorie,
whose run at the Purple Onion was ending. The idea of singing
professionally had never crossed her mind, but the manager of the
Garden of Allah had just given her notice—mainly to appease the
strippers who resented her attitude—and she needed another job.

When I was growing up in Stamps, Arkansas, Momma used
to take me to some church service every day of the week.
At each gathering we sang. So I knew I could sing, I did not
know how well. . . . I had never sung to piano accompani-
ment, and although my sense of rhythm was adequate, I had
not the shadow of an understanding of meter.

—MAYA ANGELOU, *SINGIN' AND SWINGIN' AND GETTIN' MERRY
LIKE CHRISTMAS*, RANDOM HOUSE, 1976

Her voice may have been un-trained, but when she sang "Run Joe" at that party she had enhanced her performance by bringing the story to life with her vocal delivery, expressions, movement, and dance. That spur of the moment performance convinced Marguerite's musician friends that she could do a cabaret act. They in turn convinced her that she could pull it off, worked with her on her costumes and music and provided vocal coaching. They also insisted that she needed to create a new persona or at the very least come up with a more distinctive name that would set her apart.

This photograph of Maya appeared in *Audience* magazine in May 1954 during her run at the Purple Onion. In the brief accompanying article, she is given an "exotic" and totally ficti-tious background—a "Cuban mother and a Wa-tusi father," with the writer also claiming that she spent her childhood in Cuba.
(Photo by G. Paul Bishop)

She chose the name Maya, because since childhood her brother Bailey had called her "My" or "Myah." Maya evoked the love and memories they shared. And one of her mentors suggested that An-gelos become Angelou. So Marguerite Johnson Angelos, at twenty-five, became Maya Angelou, the calypso singer. And it was Maya Angelou, who got booked at the Purple Onion and stepped into the spotlight in 1954.

Located in the North Beach neighborhood of San Francisco, a bohemian enclave, known as a haven of the Beat Generation, the club had a reputation for boosting the careers of up and coming co-medians and folk singers and the critics took notice. Phyllis Diller

shared the bill with Maya, who opened to rave reviews. The Purple Onion was a major stepping stone for Maya—performing there built her confidence, connected her to an ever-widening circle of show biz folk, and created a buzz. "Popularity was an intoxicant and I swayed drunkenly for months. . . . Fans began to recognize me in the street and one well-to-do woman organized a ten member Maya Angelou fan club" (Angelou, *Singin' and Swingin' and Gettin' Merry*).

Opportunities came knocking. Maya was invited to audition to replace Eartha Kitt in the touring company of the highly acclaimed show *New Faces of 1953*. She was asked to join the company in 1954, but her hopes were dashed when the Purple Onion refused to let her out of her contract. Little did she know when she sat entranced at a performance of *Porgy and Bess* that another door was opening. The show and its stellar cast had received nothing but raves on tour and their reception in San Francisco in 1954 was no exception. When members of the cast came to the Purple Onion to hear Maya sing they were equally lavish in their praise and at their urging Maya tried out for the company's European tour. They wanted to hire her on the spot, but because her contract with the Purple Onion wasn't up for two months, they offered the carrot that they would keep her in mind while continuing to hold auditions.

When her contract at the Purple Onion finally expired Maya had two tempting offers on her plate. The producers of a new Broadway musical *House of Flowers* had flown her to New York for

an audition and offered her a role in the show. Written by Truman Capote, with a score by Harold Arlen, choreography by George Balanchine, and a cast including Diahann Carroll, Pearl Bailey, and Josephine Premice, *House of Flowers* was destined to become a hit. While in New York Maya received the call to join the company of *Porgy and Bess,* as a principal dancer and playing the minor role of Ruby on its European tour. Two incredible opportunities but for Maya: "There really was no contest. I wanted to travel, to try to speak other languages, to see the cities I had read about all my life, but most important I wanted to be with a large, friendly group of Black people who sang so gloriously and lived with such passion" (Angelou, *Singin' and Swingin' and Gettin' Merry*).

(TOP) Maya stepping off the train in Paris with her friend and sister cast mate, Martha Flowers, and another member of the *Porgy and Bess* crew. *(Angelou-Johnson Family Archives)*

(RIGHT) When the cast of *Porgy and Bess* toured the ruins of Pompeii, Maya cavorted with the children in the company to keep them from seeing the more gruesome remains. *(Angelou-Johnson Family Archives)*

There was no time to go home; she had to join the cast immediately. It was an extraordinary opportunity but it meant that now she would be leaving her child in his grandmother's keeping. When she called home to share her news, trying to cushion the pain, she promised Clyde, who was nine, that they would not be parted for long, while all too

aware that the tour was scheduled to last nearly two years.

Despite feeling torn and guilty about leaving her son and misleading him about how long they would be parted, the *Porgy and Bess* experience is one that Maya regards as pivotal in her life. In Europe, the company was showered with praise. For Maya it was a joy to work with and learn from so many accomplished singers and actors. Years later Maya vividly recalled the show's opening night in Milan in the winter of 1955:

After leaving the *Porgy and Bess* tour, Maya boarded a New York–bound ship in Naples and immediately became the center of attention. *(Angelou-Johnson Family Archives)*

This was something unique: famous white American performers had appeared at La Scala, but never blacks, especially not a huge cast of blacks such as *Porgy* provided. Both audience and company were tense. Every member of the cast was coiled tight like a spring, wound taut for a shattering release. The moment the curtain opened, the singers pulled the elegant first-night audience into the harshness of black Southern life. The love story unfolded with such tenderness that the singers wept visible tears. Time and again, the audience came to their feet, yelling and applauding. We had performed *Porgy and Bess* as never before, and if the La Scala patrons loved us, it was only fitting because we certainly performed as if we were in love with one another.

—JAMES SANDIFER, "THE COMPLICATED LIFE OF
PORGY AND BESS," HUMANITIES, 1997

Having hungered to see the world, Maya seized every opportunity to explore and study each new place and culture, learn the language, and connect to the people. The tour took her to Yugoslavia (then part of Communist Eastern Europe) to Italy, France, Egypt, Israel, and Greece. In Paris, where the company stayed for several months, and later in Rome, she sang at popular nightclubs like Bricktop's to supplement her salary. While in Paris Maya met and immediately bonded with James Baldwin, who was living in France at the time—it was the beginning of their deep and lasting friendship. She taught American dance in Israel and Italy. She visited the pyramids, sailed on the Nile, explored the Holy Land, walked through the Acropolis soaking up history, always meeting people, always learning more about herself and the world. For the first time she was experiencing life as a Black person in societies free of the segregation and institutionalized racism that polluted America.

She'd been on tour for a year when news from home forced her to change her plans. Her mother sent a letter telling Maya that her son desperately missed and needed her. The company was in Rome when she gave her notice, and to help build her nest egg she moonlighted by singing at Bricktop's. (The club, which bore the name of the African American woman who owned it, was one of Europe's most famous cabarets.)

When she returned to America in 1955 Maya's first priority was mothering her son, reconnecting with him and solidifying their bond. She continued to sing, in clubs in California and Hawaii, but these were always short bookings and Maya often brought her son along with her. And when her bright, rambunctious ten-year-old son Clyde announced that he wished to be called Guy, his mother, who had also changed her name, honored his request. Still eager to live in the world and curious about other lifestyles Maya stopped singing and, with Guy in tow, joined a beatnik commune in Sausalito. But after a few months, missing certain creature comforts, she was both yearning for privacy and increasingly concerned that her son was "becoming animal wild."

Mother and son moved to Los Angeles. Maya rented a small bungalow in Laurel Canyon and, far more motivated than she'd ever been before, resumed her nightclub act. Her timing was perfect. It was 1956 and the country had fallen in love with calypso, Harry Belafonte was its king and in California Maya became

Maya in performance at Ye Little Club in Beverly Hills, California, in 1956. *(Photo © Chuck Stewart. All rights reserved)*

the reigning queen. She was working steadily as a singer, "I followed the jobs, and against the advice of a pompous white psychologist, I had taken Guy along. . . . When the money was plentiful, we lived in swank hotels and called room service. At other times we stayed in boardinghouses, I strung sheets as room dividers, and cooked our favorite foods illegally on a two-burner hot plate" (Maya Angelou, *The Heart of a Woman*, Random House, 1981).

Maya and Guy were comfortably settled in Los Angeles and her career was on a roll when she made her film debut in 1957 as a featured performer in the musical *Calypso Heat Wave* singing "Run, Joe." That same year she recorded the album *Miss Calypso* for Liberty Records, singing both standards and her own songs, notably "Mambo in Africa," "Neighbor, Neighbor," and "Tamo." (The LP was reissued as a CD in 1996 by Scamp Records.)

Long before she'd stepped into the spotlight as a performer, before she'd dreamed of dancing, Maya Angelou knew that words had power and had fallen in love with the written word. For years she'd been putting pen to paper and while living in Los Angeles she began to write in earnest—song lyrics at first, then poetry and short stories. She knew that singing, though it provided her a living and a bit

Langston Hughes, one of the great poets whose work inspired Maya, came to hear her sing while on a visit to Los Angeles. *(Photo © Chuck Stewart. All rights reserved)*

of fame, wasn't her calling. But it was only after meeting the author John O. Killens and sharing her work with him that the idea of seriously pursuing writing took hold.

When Killens urged her to come to New York City and join the Harlem Writers Guild, Maya Angelou once again stepped out on faith. It was 1959 and the winds of change were beginning to roar across the nation when Maya and Guy moved to Brooklyn.

The Guild had been founded in 1950 by a group of Black writers, including Killens, the historian John Henrik Clarke, and novelist Rosa Guy, to encourage, develop, and champion the work of Black writers. At the Guild's meetings, hosted in the home of one the members, aspiring and published writers shared their work and received needed critique. Invariably the group discussed and debated the issues of the day, foremost among them the push for African independence and the Black liberation struggles at home and abroad.

The value of the Harlem Writers Guild sessions is captured in the reminiscences of Maya's son, Guy Johnson, who in addition to being a novelist, is also a poet:

A poster advertising *Calypso Heat Wave* (1957), the movie in which Maya made her screen debut singing and dancing.

My first memories of writing, its creative processes and the work required to master it as a craft began in New York when my mother would host meetings of the Harlem Writers Guild. I guess I was about thirteen or fourteen and I would listen furtively at the slightly ajar door of my bedroom as people read stories or new sections of work in progress. I was intrigued by what was read as well as the conversations, which ensued. Often points were debated hotly as people challenged and defended characters, story lines and overall philosophical perspectives.

—GUY JOHNSON, *CONTEMPORARY AUTHORS ONLINE*, GUYJOHNSONBOOKS.COM

At their best, writers' groups serve as nurturing incubators and tough crucibles for their members. At Maya's first reading the group put her feet to the fire. She read a one-act play she'd titled *One Love, One Life*. "Even as I read I knew the drama was bad, but maybe someone would have lied a little." That hope was quickly dashed when John Henrik Clarke exclaimed "*One Life. One Love*? I found very little life and very little love in the play from the opening of the act to its unfortunate end" (Angelou, *The Heart of a Woman*).

Although he eviscerated her play, Clarke made it clear that he was delighted that she had joined the group. The feedback she received that night pushed her to acknowledge that "I had taken words and the art of arranging them too lightly. The writers assaulted my casual approach and made me confront my intention. If I wanted to write, I had to develop a level of concentration found mostly in people awaiting execution. I had to learn technique and surrender my ignorance" (Angelou, *The Heart of a Woman*).

And so began her arduous journey to become a writer. She would spend years writing and rewriting poetry, plays, short stories, and essays, constantly honing her skills, exploring different forms and styles, sharpening her concentration, finding her true voice. As a member of the Guild not only was Maya honing her skills as a writer, she was establishing friendships with Killens and Clarke, Rosa Guy, Paule Marshall, Julian Mayfield, and so many other fellow writers that would last a lifetime.

for a few month I was a novelt
Then the after dance began to watch
I was told that people had gone
other club to listen to a real singer
curiosity led me. Then came a Nig
Then there was a decided drop in
business. Night after night attend
began to wane until it became
common to find the club only a
full at showtime I was told th
a rival had hired an
authentic singer. I went alone to
to see my competition and th
show made me come to
grips with my life.

Della Reese was announced an
Then she appeared there was an
audible gasp. She was nearly six feet
tall and very beautiful and wa
wearing what could be called a pro
gown. There were no sequins or bea
or phony stars on her dress. She was
certainly not dressed in costume. Sh

CHAPTER 3

Changing the World

*I'd like to be thought of as someone who tried to be
a blessing rather than a curse on the human race.*

—MAYA ANGELOU (1993)

❧

for a few month I was a novelty
then ... attendance began to wane
... was told that people had gone
...ther close to listen to a real singer
...riosity led me. Then came a ...
...en there was a decided drop in
...siveness. Night after night attendance
began to wane until it became
common to find the club only a...
...ll at showtime I was told the
...rival had hired an ...
...thentic singer. I went alone to ...
...to see my competition and th...
...spot ... show made me come to
grips with my life.
Della Reese was announced an...
...hen she appeared there was an
...dible gasp. She was nearly six feet
...ll and very beautiful and was...
...aking what could be called a pro...
...own. There were no sequins or bea...
...or shiny stars on her dress. She was
...tainly not dressed in costume...

WHEN MAYA MOVED TO NEW YORK in 1959, the long struggle to end racial oppression had caught fire. Movements challenging Colonialism in Africa and the Caribbean and demanding independence were gaining ground, while in the United States the Civil Rights movement was building momentum.

The freedom train was gathering speed and Maya Angelou was eager to get onboard. She had spent her childhood in the segregated South, where her sense of justice and equity first took root: "I was always concerned about justice and injustice. To the extent that I could understand the issues, I was always on the side of the underdog. I'm on the same side today" (Jeffrey M. Elliot, "Maya Angelou Raps").

She was among the congregation when Martin Luther King Jr. came to a church in Harlem to rally support for the southern movement to end segregation. His lyrically powerful oratory, the sureness of his faith, his belief that America could be redeemed, and his "prophetic litany" awed and inspired and challenged all who heard him speak on that early summer night in 1960. After hearing King, Maya and her friend, the superbly talented comedian and actor Godfrey Cambridge, sprang into action. Calling on the talents of many of their fellow performers, within a few short weeks they produced a show to raise money for King's Southern Christian Leadership Conference (SCLC). The revue, *Cabaret for Freedom*, which in addition to coproducing, Maya also wrote, ran for five weeks at the Village Gate in New York City. It was a huge success and Maya's organizational skills so impressed Bayard Rustin, the director of the SCLC's New York office, that when he announced that he was resigning he asked her to take his place. Rustin was a brilliant activist and intellectual and a towering figure in the Movement. It was an enormous compliment and powerful challenge. To accept meant walking away from her career as a performer, something she'd worked hard to build and sustain. Her repertoire now ranged the African diaspora including the blues, calypso, Afro-Cuban chants, and South African freedom songs. She'd wowed the crowd at Harlem's legendary Apollo Theater, and was being steadily booked for local and out-of-town gigs in cabarets. She was a budding playwright and poet. But the call to activism proved impossible to resist.

Maya, in her new role as the Northeastern Regional Coordinator in the SCLC's New York office, quickly proved Rustin right in his assessment of her organizational, public relations, and fundraising skills. Her work so impressed the group's leaders that Dr. King made a point of coming to meet her. "He was shorter than I expected and so young. He had an easy friendliness, which was unsettling. Looking at him in my office, alone, was like seeing a lion sitting down at my dining room table eating a plate of mustard greens" (Angelou, *The Heart of a Woman*).

During the course of that first meeting King asked about her family and she found herself talking about her "brilliant" beloved brother, Bailey. Time and again his ambitions had been thwarted, and the death of his first wife had sent him on a downward spiral. "The personal sadness he showed when I spoke of my brother put my heart in his keeping forever" (Angelou, *The Heart of a Woman*).

But Maya's activism extended beyond her work with the SCLC. In many ways Maya, who was already insisting on being called Black rather than Negro, was far more radical than many of her SCLC colleagues. While others feared being labeled Communist, she along with many members of the Harlem Writers Guild championed the Cuban revolution. When Fidel Castro and his delegation, who'd come to attend the United Nations opening session in 1960, were kicked out of a midtown hotel they were invited to stay at the Hotel Theresa in Harlem. Maya left her desk at the SCLC to join the huge crowd that turned out to welcome Castro.

Just as she championed fair play for Cuba, Maya was also becoming more knowledgeable and outspoken in her support of the African freedom struggles. The Sharpeville Massacre in South Africa in 1960 marked the beginning of Maya's anti-apartheid activism. But she never imagined that she was about to embark on a journey of the heart when she attended a gathering at the Killenses' apartment in support of the South African freedom struggle. She had put in a long day at the SCLC office and almost didn't go, but her friends and her activist son, who had heard him speak at other events, had been praising one of the evening's honored guests, a South African freedom fighter named Vusumi (Vus) Make. The sparks that flew between them when they met took her by surprise. They were physical opposites; Vus was overweight and shorter than she by several inches. None of that mattered, he radiated self-confidence, and listening to him speak, Maya was totally captivated by his intelligence, vision, and passion. "When he finished, he asked

Maya shown here with her "husband," Vusumi Make, the South African anti-apartheid activist whom she met and fell in love with in New York City while working for the Southern Christian Leadership Conference. *(Angelou-Johnson Family Archives)*

for questions and sat down, dabbing at his face with a cloud of white handkerchief. My first reaction was to wish that I could be the white cloth in his dark hand touching his forehead, digging softly in the corners of his lips" (Angelou, *The Heart of a Woman*).

The attraction was mutual, Vus made it clear that Maya Angelou was the woman he'd been waiting for. But Maya was engaged to another man—a solid, relatively successful bail bondsman named Thomas Allen, whom she'd been seeing for months. Despite knowing that other than their mutual enjoyment of "sex and good food" they had little in common, Maya agreed to marry him. She'd made a pragmatic decision. As Mrs. Allen she would be assured a stable, secure life. Her wedding was just a few months away. But despite all her carefully laid plans she was immediately drawn to the charming, charismatic South African.

Vus embarked on a campaign to woo and win her, lavishing his attention on both Maya and Guy. He swept her away. Within a matter of weeks, she'd broken her engagement and, with her son's blessing, agreed to marry Vus Make, who whisked Maya off to London, where they attended a conference of African nationalists. He wanted them to marry in England. She wanted to wed with her family present. They decided to simply tell everyone that they were married and planned to work out the details later, but they never got around to officially tying the knot.

When Maya returned to New York everyone assumed that she and Vus were married. The new family settled into an apartment in Manhattan. Though frequently on the road soliciting support for the South African freedom struggle Vus was an attentive husband and Maya loved seeing him bond with Guy. But Vus also held rigidly traditional views about marriage. He was adamant about her not working and to please him she resigned her position at the SCLC.

Even if Vus had not asked, Maya probably would have left the SCLC on her own accord. Her position had been seriously undermined. Two White men had been hired and more and more of her responsibilities were being turned over to them. When she resigned, Stanley Levinson, the director of the New York office, informed her that the two men had been hired because it was always assumed that she would resume her career as a performer.

Now Maya's full-time job became being Mrs. Make. Vus loved showing her off, and expected her to excel as his hostess. Maya soon found herself working almost nonstop to keep their home up to her

Maya singing for friends at an impromptu gathering. *(Angelou-Johnson Family Archives)*

"husband's" super-meticulous standards. But she never stopped being an activist. With several of her sister writers from the Guild, she organized the Cultural Association for Women of African Heritage (CAWAH) in January 1961 to support the work of all Civil Rights groups.

The group was passionately committed to supporting human rights at home and abroad, especially Africa's struggles for independence. With Maya and her sister friend Rosa Guy leading the charge, CAWAH sprang into action when Patrice Lumumba, the first prime minister of the newly independent Republic of the Congo, was assassinated. After being ousted in a coup orchestrated by the CIA and the Belgians because he refused to toady to his country's former colonial masters, Lumumba had been murdered in January 1961. News of his execution set off waves of protests, and CAWAH played a prominent role in organizing and leading demonstrations at the United Nations.

Many established Civil Rights leaders, leery of Lumumba's alleged Communist ties, criticized the women of CAWAH for being too radical and condemned the demonstrations. But Maya and Rosa had convinced CAWAH to organize the protest after hearing Malcolm X, the Nation of Islam spokesman, denounce the assassination. When he refused to support the demonstration the two women sought him out. At their meeting Malcolm X explained that he was opposed to any pleadings before a racist tribunal during their meeting. Maya was so overwhelmed by his presence that she was almost at a loss for words: "His aura was too bright and his masculine force affected me physically. . . . He approached, and all my brain would do for me was record his coming. I have never been so affected by a human presence. Up close he was a great red arch through which one could pass to eternity" (Angelou, *The Heart of a Woman*). Although she barely spoke at that meeting, Maya and Malcolm were destined to make an intellectual and emotional connection.

Despite the criticism they received from some quarters, the interrelationship between the independence struggles in Africa and the freedom movement in America was clear to Maya and her CAWAH sisters and many of her fellow Guild members.

Her husband was supportive of her work with CAWAH, viewing her activism as a complement to his own. But the idea of Mrs. Make stepping back out on stage was not on the agenda, so when Maya was asked to do a reading of Jean Genet's play *The Blacks*, she did it as a favor. The play was being mounted Off-Broadway at the St. Mark's Theatre in Greenwich Village and her friends Max Roach and his wife, Abbey Lincoln, were involved in the production. Max, already a jazz legend, had composed the music. And Abbey, a superb singer and actor, who'd become one of Maya's close sister-friends when they were both living in L.A. years before, was slated to play one of the lead roles. Like Maya, Abbey was also a budding writer and a passionate activist and the two were close confidantes.

When Max asked her to do the reading with Abbey when he presented his music to the producers, Maya couldn't refuse. But, other than the music, Maya found nothing about the play appealing: "I thought *The Blacks* was a White foreigner's idea of a people he did not understand." When she received a call offering her a role, her immediate response was to say no. But she still bridled when Vus summarily dismissed the idea of his wife performing on stage. When Vus abruptly changed his tune after he read the play Maya

SHOWBILL
THE BLACKS

Showbill cover and cast listing for *The Blacks.* Maya played the White Queen in this award-winning Off-Broadway production of Jean Genet's classic work about the impact of racism. Cicely Tyson, Godfrey Cambridge, Louis Gossett, James Earl Jones, Roscoe Lee Browne, and several other members of this all-Black cast went on to become stars of both the stage and the screen. Theatergoers would later flock to see plays written by Charles Gordone, another cast mate. Most of the members of this cast became Maya's lifelong friends.

CLOSE-UPS

ETHEL AYLER (Augusta Snow) was in Broadway productions of *Jamaica* with Lena Horne and *The Cool World*. Last season she was seen as Carmen in the Thearte-in-the-Park production of *Carmen Jones*, and she has toured for several seasons in *Porgy and Bess* and *Carmen Jones*.

CYNTHIA BELGRAVE (Adelaide Bobo), since coming to New York in 1957, was in the original Broadway cast of *Raisin in the Sun*. Her other New York credits include important roles in *Take A Giant Step*, *Simply Heavenly*, *Three By O'Neill*, *And the Wind Blows* and *Wingless Victory*. She has appeared on the screen in *Odds Against Tomorrow*, *A Matter of Conviction* and *Something Wild in the City*.

ROSCOE LEE BROWNE (Archibald Wellington) made his New York stage début with the New York Shakespeare Festival, appearing in *Julius Caesar*, *Romeo and Juliet*, *Titus Andronicus* and understudying *Othello*. He received excellent personal notices for his portrayal of the dope tycoon in *The Cool World* on Broadway. Since then he has appeared in *The Pretender*, *Dark of the Moon* and in the Toronto company of *The Connection*. He is also featured in the film of *The Connection*.

GODFREY M. CAMBRIDGE (Diouf) first appeared on Broadway in Herman Wouk's *Nature's Way*. He was featured in *Lost in the Stars* for the City Center and in the off-Broadway production of *Take A Giant Step*. He was most recently seen as Lou Brody in the E.L.T. production of *Detective Story*. Mr Cambridge has been seen on television on the Phil Silvers Show, Search for Tomorrow, Ellery Queen and featured on Naked City. In the film *The Last Angry Man* he was seen as Nobody Home, a juvenile hoodlum.

CHARLES GORDONE (Valet) is an actor, director and singer. Broadway audiences have seen him in *Mrs. Patterson* and *The Climate of Eden* in the role of Logan, which he recently recreated in the television version on the Play of the Week. He has directed plays for the Judson Studio Players. His direction of *Detective Story* this season at Equity Library Theatre received excellent reviews by the critics. He has toured the country as a folk and Calypso singer.

LOUIS GOSSETT (Edgar Alas Newport News) can currently be seen in the movie version of *Raisin in the Sun*, recreating the part he originated in the Broadway production. He has been seen on Broadway in *Desk Set*, *Take A Giant Step* and at City Center in *Lost in the Stars*. His television appearances include roles on Big Story, Omnibus, Suspicion and You Are There. He has recorded a folk-singing album which is soon to be released.

JAMES EARL JONES (Deodatus Village) was seen on Broadway in *The Egghead*, *Sunrise at Campobello* and *The Cool World*. Off-Broadway he was seen in *The Pretender* and N. Y. Shakespeare Festival productions of *Henry V*, *Measure for Measure* and *Romeo and Juliet*. He made his New York stage début portraying Sgt. Blunt in *Wedding in Japan*. On television he has been seen as one of Phil Silvers platoon in the Sgt. Bilko Show.

MAYA ANGELOU MAKE (Queen) is making her legitimate début in *The Blacks*. She has played the dance lead of Ruby in *Porgy and Bess*. She has worked the night club circuit, appearing in New York at the Village Vanguard, Blue Angel, Le Cupidon and at the Hungry i in San Francisco. A choreographer as well, Miss Make has choreographed two movies, *Juke Box Jamboree* and *Calypso Heatwave*.

HELEN MARTIN (Felicity Trollop Pardon) appeared earlier this season on Broadway in Tennessee Williams' *Period of Adjustment*. Other Broadway credits include *Take A Giant Step*, *Native Son*, *The Long Dream* and *Deep Are the Roots* which she also played in London, Scotland and Wales. Off-Broadway audiences have seen

9

ST. MARKS PLAYHOUSE

Sidney Bernstein, George Edgar and Andre Gregory
BY ARRANGEMENT WITH GERALDINE LUST
present

Jean Genet's

THE BLACKS

Directed by
Gene Frankel
Translated by Bernard Frechtman

Ethel Ayler · Charles Gordone · Lex Monson · Cynthia Belgrave · Louis Gossett · Roscoe Lee Browne · James Earl Jones · Maya Angelou Make · Jay J. Riley · Raymond St. Jacques · Godfrey M. Cambridge · Helen Martin · Cicely Tyson

Sets by Kim E. Swados
Movement by Talley Beatty
Lighting by Lee Watson
Music Supervised by Charles Gross
Costumes and Masks by Patricia Zipprodt
Production Stage Mgr. Maxwell Glanville
Production Associate Alfred Manacher

CAST
(In order of appearance)

Archibald Wellington	Roscoe Lee Browne
Deodatus Village	James Earl Jones
Adelaide Bobo	Cynthia Belgrave
Edgar Alas Newport News	Louis Gossett
Augusta Snow	Ethel Ayler
Felicity Trollop Pardon	Helen Martin
Stephanie Virtue Diop	Cicely Tyson
Diouf	Godfrey M. Cambridge
Missionary	Lex Monson
Judge	Raymond St. Jacques
Governor	Jay J. Riley
Queen	Maya Angelou Make
Valet	Charles Gordone
Drummer	Charles Campbell

There will be one ten minute intermission.

was stunned. Where she took umbrage at the play's assumption that given the opportunity Blacks would behave as cruelly as Whites, he saw it as clear warning about how power corrupts and insisted that she do the play.

Maya was given the role of the White Queen in Genet's surrealistic meditation on colonialism, where the "colonized" imitate their oppressors by taking on many of their worst traits. She joined a stellar group of actors: in addition to Abbey Lincoln, the cast included Cicely Tyson, James Earl Jones, Roscoe Lee Browne, Louis Gossett, Godfrey Cambridge, Charles Gordone, and Raymond St. Jacques: "I started enjoying my role. I used the White Queen to ridicule mean white women and brutal white men who had too often injured me and mine. Every inane posture and haughty attitude I had ever seen found its place in my White Queen" (Angelou, *The Heart of a Woman*).

It was 1961 and, given the play's scathing portrayal of White attitudes and behavior, Maya never expected it to be well received. Then things got really dicey when Max, embroiled in a bitter dispute with the producers, pulled his music within hours of opening night, and Abbey withdrew from the cast in support of her husband. After making sure that their friendship would not be jeopardized Maya remained with the play and, in collaboration with Ethel Ayler, who replaced Abbey in the cast, quickly wrote two songs for the production. To Maya's surprise, the play garnered rave reviews, as did her performance. But after the show had been up and running for several months, the producers refused to properly acknowledge the work she and Ethel had done, so Maya quit.

Ironically it was while she was performing in *The Blacks* that

Maya became the target of an escalating campaign of surveillance and harassment by agents of South Africa's apartheid regime, who considered her husband an enemy of the state. She began to receive threatening phone calls: voices whispering that her husband was in jeopardy or dead made her worry about his safety. Then someone called claiming that Guy had been gravely injured and was in the hospital. She panicked only to discover that it was a cruel hoax: "I had opposed the racist regime on principle, because it was ugly, violent, debasing and murderous. But . . . to break a mother's heart for no gain was the most squalid act I could imagine. My defiance from now on would be personal" (Angelou, *The Heart of a Woman*).

Those threatening phone calls also made her even more determined to stay with Vus. But much as she loved her husband and believed in his work, she had serious concerns about their relationship. Vus spent money lavishly, often left important bills unpaid and refused to discuss their finances with his "wife." His imperious attitude about a woman's place grated on her and she had come to suspect that he was being unfaithful. Yet, despite her growing unease, Maya was still determined to try to make a go of her marriage. They had been together less than a year and she was still feeling her way when Vus announced that they were moving to Cairo where he was to be the delegate of the South African United Front. Maya put her reservations aside and packed their bags. It was 1961 and Africa was calling.

⊂꜒⊃⨯⊂⊃

for a few month I was a novelty
then attendance began to wane
I was told that people had gone
other club to listen to a real singer
curiosity led me. Then came a night
when there was a decided drop in
business. Night after night, often da...
began to wane until it became
common to find the club only at
... at showtime I was told that
rival ... had hired an
authentic singer. I went alone to ...
... My competition and the
... show made me come to
grips with my life.

Della Reese was announced an...
when she appeared there was an
incredible gasp. She was nearly six feet
tall and very beautiful and was
making what could be called a pro...
...ion. There were no sequins or bea...
or shiny stars on her dress. She was
certainly not ... no costumed ...

CHAPTER 4

A Daughter Returns

*I believe that it's wise for all of us to keep in mind
that we're in process, and to keep on our traveling
shoes. Nobody's here to stay. We're in process.*

—MAYA ANGELOU (1985)

for a few month I was a novelty
then the attendance began to wane
I was told that people had come
close to listen to a real singer
riosity led me. Then came a Nigh
en there was a decided drop. Aft
iveness. Night after night attenda
egan to wane until it became
mon to find the club over at
ll at showtime I was told tha
rival had hired an
thentic singer. I went alone to
to see my competition and the
pa show made me come to
    reps with my life.
    Della Reese was announced an
hen she appeared there was an
dible gasp. She was nearly six feet
ll and very beautiful and was
aring what could be called a gro
wn. There were no sequins or bea
r phony stars on her dress. She was
tainly not dressed in costume

WHEN MAYA ANGELOU PACKED HER BAGS to join her husband in Egypt in 1961 she was part of a vanguard of Black American artists and intellectuals who were choosing to make Africa their home. During the four years that she lived on the continent—especially her time in Ghana—she came to fully recognize that Africa had always been with her. It was imprinted in the fabric of Black Stamps, in the games she played as a child, the folktales elders shared. It influenced sensibilities and behavior, the grave formality of elders in Ghana so like her Grandmother Henderson's demeanor.

It was alive in the spoken and body language of Black America, in the music and the kitchen.

Maya's African sojourn began in Cairo where Vus Make had been sent to represent the South African United Front. She delighted in the city. And Guy at sixteen took to living in Cairo with gusto, becoming increasingly more involved

In 1962 Maya and her son, Guy, left the United States to join Vus Make in Cairo, where they became part of the sub-Saharan African diplomatic community. Here she greets a southern African freedom fighter at one of the many receptions she attended while living there. *(Angelou-Johnson Family Archives)*

with school, his new circle of friends, and exploring the city. The Makes were a gregarious, charismatic duo and their home quickly became a gathering place for African activists, diplomats, and intellectuals.

Vus was frequently away, traveling throughout the continent as an emissary for the anti-apartheid movement and going on dangerous underground missions. He was a brilliant man engaged in important work on behalf of the South African struggle and Maya was proudly supportive of him. But she was also a woman used to doing her own work and being recognized and respected in her own right. And the problems that had begun to surface when they were living in New York soon became impossible to ignore.

In their circle of African diplomats and activists it was assumed that the men paid the bills and the wives remained in the home. But Vus tended to ignore his family's mounting debts. When the bill collectors began beating a path to their door, while he was off on one of his trips, Maya decided she could no longer play the dutiful wife. She was going to get a job. Her need to ensure a secure home far outweighed her husband's outrage and hurt feelings. She turned to a journalist friend, David Du Bois, to aid in her quest. Black Americans far from home, the two had struck up an almost immediate brother-sister friendship. DuBois, the stepson of the revered African American activist and intellectual W. E. B. Du Bois, was a well connected journalist and a lecturer at Cairo University. He arranged an interview for Maya with an Egyptian colleague who was starting an English-language magazine, the *Arab Observer*.

Although she had no experience Maya was hired as an associate editor. Not only was she stepping into unknown territory, she would also be the lone female editor on the staff.

> I got the Africa Desk–Politics. It was really interesting, because I was, at once, a female, non-Muslim, non-Arab, American, Black, and six feet tall. All I needed was that I should be Jewish! It was a shock to the community. It was really terrifying that each time I spoke, each time the magazine came out, there was the question of: Was that my point of view, or was I speaking for my husband? . . . All the other journalists were male and the idea of having a woman even work there, let alone a woman as boss, was ridiculous. But we worked it out.
>
> —JUDITH RICH, "LIFE IS FOR LIVING," *WESTWAYS*,
> SEPTEMBER 1987

She had bluffed her way into the job by inflating her skills to impress her friend, and DuBois had further embellished them. Once hired, she had to really learn how to swim. Assigned to cover sub-Saharan Africa she immediately embarked on a crash course in journalism, while simultaneously mining every available source to gain greater fluency and knowledge about Black Africa and working to gain the trust and respect of her male colleagues. In *The Heart of a Woman* she recalled: "I stayed at the *Observer* for over a year and gradually my ignorance receded." She became adept at writing and editing articles for the magazine and learned the nuances of layout and design. Her work was recognized and rewarded, "I received a raise from Dr. Nagati [my boss], the respect of my fellow workers and a few compliments from strangers."

She was working long hours, her salary keeping their household afloat. Her marriage, however, was foundering. Vus, though still proclaiming that he loved her, no longer attempted to mask his infidelities. It was a painful period, but Maya had established deep and abiding friendships that were a source of both joy and solace. In addition to her brother-friend David Du Bois, she had bonded with three African women—Hanifa Fathy, A. B. Williamson, and Kebi Endatchew. Hanifa, an Egyptian whose husband was a high-ranking judge, was a member of Cairo's privileged class. But contrary to custom she had established her own identity as an acclaimed poet. Maya and the witty, spirited Hanifa had quickly discovered that they were kindred spirits. A. B. Williamson, a Liberian, and Kebi Endatchew, from Ethiopia, were married to diplomats from their respective countries. The effervescent A.B., called Banti by her friends, and the beautiful, reserved Kebi had reached out to Maya when she arrived in Cairo. They helped her find her bearings within the rather insular world of the African diplomatic colony, provided valuable insights about women's lives in sub-Saharan Africa, and made it their mission to introduce her to other Black African women.

Friendships aside, by the spring of 1962, there was little to keep Maya in Cairo. Her relationship with Vus had permanently soured. The last of her love and trust had been eroded by his blatant infidelities. Guy, newly graduated from high school, was eager to attend the University of Ghana in Accra. And anti-American feelings were on the rise in Egypt and Maya was feeling increasingly unwelcome at the *Observer*, where she was the lone American.

Although she decided to leave Cairo she was determined to remain in Africa. Enlisting the help of Joe Williamson, her friend Banti's diplomat husband, Maya was offered a job with the Department of Information in Liberia. Eager to explore West Africa, she planned to stop in Ghana, enroll Guy at the University in Accra, help him get settled, and then continue on to Monrovia.

The moment she stepped foot in Accra, Ghana's capital city, in the summer of 1962, she felt like she'd come home. "Guy was seventeen and quick. I was thirty-three and determined. We were Black Americans in West Africa, where for the first time in our lives the color of our skin was accepted as correct and normal" (Maya Angelou, *All God's Children Need Traveling Shoes,* Random House, 1986).

Maya and Guy were immediately welcomed by a group of Black American expatriates—chief among them the writer Julian Mayfield and his physician wife, Anna Livia Cordero, friends from Maya's Harlem Writers Guild days—all of whom urged her to remain in Ghana. Though she was tempted, there was a job waiting for her in Liberia. But within days of their arrival all of her carefully laid plans were thrown aside when Guy was critically injured in a car accident, his neck broken in three places, an arm and a leg fractured. The doctors informed her that her son, who'd been immobilized in a body cast,

Ghana embraced Maya like a long-lost daughter and she returned the love. Here she's serenading a group of Ghanaian friends at a party. *(Angelou-Johnson Family Archives)*

would be in the hospital for two months and faced several more months of recovery at home. Consumed with worry about Guy, she spent every day by his side in the hospital and brooded alone, in self-imposed isolation every night in her room.

> I moved into the YWCA, and wrote to Joe and Banti
> Williamson. Going to Liberia had to be canceled. I would
> find a job and stay in Ghana. Anna Livia allowed me to use
> her kitchen to cook daily meals for Guy. I hitchhiked, found
> rides, or took the mammy lorry (jitney service) to the hospi-
> tal. My money was leaking away and I had to find work.
>
> —ANGELOU, *THE HEART OF A WOMAN*

Yet depression was eroding that fierce, "I Can" spirit of hers just when she needed it most. She was feeling increasingly more overwhelmed and isolated when Julian Mayfield extended a lifeline. Reminding her that she wasn't a quitter, he announced that she needed a woman to talk to and took her to meet Efua Sutherland, the head of Ghana's National Theatre, and a poet and playwright as well. Welcoming Maya with open arms as her sister-friend, Efua encouraged her to cry and share her pain and, assuring her that she was not alone, made her a member of her family.

Having embraced Maya as her sister, Efua set about smoothing her road. Knowing that her sister needed a job she arranged a meeting with her friend J. H. Nketia, the chairman of the Institute of African Studies at the University of Ghana. He immediately offered Maya a job. It was administrative work and it didn't pay a lot, but a car came with the job. And thanks to Efua, Maya had the loan of a house for three months, time enough for Guy to complete his recovery.

Two months after being discharged from the hospital, Guy, still wearing a neck brace, enrolled in the university and moved into a dormitory, and Maya's spirits were once again soaring. She and Guy now had a Ghanian family—he an aunt, she a sister in Efua Sutherland, whose daughters embraced her as their American auntie. She was also feeling very much at home in the midst of a growing community of Black American expatriates, chief among them the Mayfield's. "I called the group 'Revolutionist Returnees.' Each person had brought to Africa varying talents, energies, vigor, youth, and terrible yearnings to be accepted" (Angelou, *All God's Children Need Traveling Shoes*).

Most of her compatriots had been drawn to Ghana because of its politics and by its charismatic leader Kwame Nkrumah's assurance of welcome. Fate had brought Maya there and though she admired Nkrumah, it was the people of Ghana that captured her: "Their skins were the colors of my childhood cravings: peanut butter, licorice, chocolate, and caramel. Theirs was the laughter of home, quick and without artifice. The erect and graceful walk of

Maya (far left) with one of her roommates, Alice Windom (far right), posing with friends at a party in Accra. The two women were part of a close circle of African American expatriates living in Ghana in the early 1960s. *(Angelou-Johnson Family Archives)*

the women reminded me of my Arkansas grandmother. . . . So I
had finally come home" (Angelou, *All God's Children Need Traveling Shoes*).

Maya and two of her "Revolutionist" friends, Vicki Garvin and
Alice Windom, pooled their money and rented a house together.
Garvin, a union organizer and trained economist, had come to
Africa hoping to put her skills to work. Despite being thwarted at
every turn, her determination to live in Ghana never dimmed.
Maya's other housemate, Alice Windom, a sociologist, was drawn
to Ghana hoping to work with others in her field. Instead, like
Garvin, who worked as a typist in an embassy, she spent her days

working as a receptionist. Of the
three, Maya had not come to Ghana
harboring any illusions about the ease
of her welcome or with a dream of
applying her skills to the work of nation building. But, having survived
baptisms by fire, the three women
were committed to living in West
Africa and to immersing themselves
in the customs and cultures of the
people and building friendships that
would bridge the divide.

The early 1960s was a period of
great hope and promise in Ghana.
The economy was flourishing and Kwame
Nkrumah was revered at home and respected abroad as a visionary
leader. A committed pan-Africanist, Nkrumah, who had studied at

Pennsylvania's historically Black Lincoln University, called out to Black Americans and West Indians to come to Ghana and contribute to the nation building. He invited the great W. E. B. Du Bois to live in Ghana and provided support for his last major project, the *Encyclopedia Africana*.

> In Ghana I was called the child who has returned home. I wore African clothes, and I learned to speak a few African languages, including Fanti. Because of my accent people thought I was from the Gambia. When I said I was American they would say, "No, no, tell the truth. What are you, where are you from? You must be Bambara." Then when I proved I was American, they said "Aah, a child who has returned home."
>
> —STEPHANIE CARUANA, "MAYA ANGELOU: AN INTERVIEW"

Much as Maya loved Ghana, home was still America. She and her fellow expatriates avidly sought to keep up with the news, discussing and debating the tactics and policies of the varying factions engaged in the freedom movement back in the States. When word of the March on Washington reached them in the summer of 1963 they decided to march on the U.S. Embassy on the same day. "The March on Washington was to begin at 7:00 A.M. on August 27. Because of the seven-hour time difference, we planned to begin our supportive march at midnight on the twenty-sixth." Shortly after the group assembled they learned that W. E. B. Du Bois, who in 1903 declared that "the problem of the 20th Century is the problem of the color line," had died. For Maya the march evoked a range of bittersweet emotions about her homeland, its promise and its denial.

But living in Ghana also tested her mettle as she struggled to stay financially afloat. At the university, Maya spent her days typing and filing, the pay barely covered her needs. To help supplement her income she worked as a freelance writer for the *Ghanaian Times.* Although the fees were meager, she was getting to use her hard-won skills as a journalist. Her distinctive voice and style as a writer and the depth and intelligence of her work soon brought wider attention. She was asked to become a features editor for the *African Review* and to do on-air work and writing for Radio Ghana. The Ghanaian Press Club invited her to become a member, an honor extended to only one other Black American writer, her friend Julian

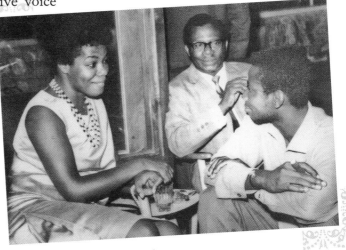

Maya left Vus Make and Egypt in 1963 and settled in Accra, Ghana, where Guy had enrolled at the university. While living in Ghana, Maya wrote for a number of local publications. *(Angelou-Johnson Family Archives)*

Mayfield. And to her heart's delight she began working at the National Theatre, where her sister Efua held sway, doing any and every task that came her way from sewing costumes, coaching students, moving sets and selling tickets, to playing the lead role in a production of Bertolt Brecht's *Mother Courage.*

In the midst of juggling her many jobs, Maya's social life was blossoming. She had a strong and growing circle of friends and a coterie of male admirers. Men tended to flock around this tall eye-catching beauty, and that she was an African American, a performing artist and writer, and an independent woman made her all the more desirable. One man in particular, a magnetic, imposing, powerful leader of one of Ghana's major ethnic groups captured her heart. They were more than a couple but not quite husband and wife. He wanted more. She loved him but still resisted taking that final step, fearful of being smothered, of losing herself. She loved him but rarely mentions him by name and keeps most of her memories about their relationship private.

Though she was busy and in love, America was very much on Maya's mind in the spring of 1964. The Black expatriate community was abuzz with excitement and bursting with pride. Malcolm X, who had taken the name El-Hajj Malik el-Shabazz after visiting Mecca, was in West Africa meeting many of its leaders and being treated as if he were a visiting head of state. It was early May when he came to Ghana. Maya's group rushed to greet him and to serve as his unofficial aides. During the course of Malcolm's visit Maya got to know him well. She was impressed by his intelligence and moved and inspired by his compassion and humility, his visionary thinking and fierce commitment to Black people. A friendship was kindled and grew stronger during the months that followed as their conversation flowed in their letters.

Maya's life in Ghana had taken on a familiar rhythm, save for one sour note. Her relationship with Guy had become somewhat strained when he began seeing a woman she heartily disapproved of. Maya had already come to the conclusion that she needed to distance herself when she received a cable from New York City informing her that the original company of *The Blacks* was being booked to appear in Berlin at the Venice Biennale and the producers were offering her a salary and a ticket. Maya leapt at the offer, and added Egypt to her itinerary so that she could see her friends in Cairo. She had a ball renewing her friendship with Roscoe Lee Browne and other members of the original cast, catching up on all the news, stretching in rehearsals, exploring Berlin and Venice. And on her way home she stopped in Cairo where her sister-friends and their families welcomed her back into the fold. When she returned to Ghana her son met her with flowers and a declaration of his independence. He assured her that he loved her and then announced that she "had finished mothering a child. You did a very good job. Now, I am a man" (Angelou, *All God's Children Need Traveling Shoes*).

Guy would always be her son, but he needed to be his own man. What did she need? In the months that followed Maya began to question her reasons for remaining in Ghana. She loved the country and its people, but she was an American. In his letters Malcolm X shared his hopes for the Organization of Afro-American Unity (OAAU) that he had founded. And when he wrote asking if she would consider returning to the United States and becoming the coordinator of the OAAU, Maya said yes.

> It seemed that I had gotten all Africa had to give me. I had
> met people and made friends. . . . I had gotten to know and
> love the children of Africa. . . . they had given me their af-
> fection and instructed me on the positive power of literally
> knowing one's place. . . . I had listened to African priests
> implore God in rhythm and voices that carried me back to

Calvary Baptist Church in San Francisco. If the heart of Africa had proved allusive, my search for it had brought me closer to understanding myself and other human beings.

—ANGELOU, *ALL GOD'S CHILDREN NEED TRAVELING SHOES*

CHAPTER 5

Blazing New Trails

*If the future road looks ominous or unpromising,
and the roads back uninviting, then we need to
gather our resolve and carrying only the necessary
baggage, step off that road in a new direction.*

—MAYA ANGELOU (2002)

for a few month I was a novelty then the attendance began to wane I was told that people had come other close to listen to a real singer riosity led me. Then came a ngu... in there was a decided drop. Af eseness. Night after night attenda egan to wane until it became mmon to find the club only a ll at showtime I was told tha rival ____ had hired an ____ thentic singer. I went alone to ... to ____ my competition and the spa ____ show made me come to eps with my life.

Della Reese was announced an hen she ____ appeared there was an dible gasp. She was nearly six feet ll and very beautiful and was ____ earing what could be called a pro own. There were no sequins or bea r phony stars on her dress. She was tainly not dressed in costume for

THE AMERICA MAYA ANGELOU returned to in February 1965 was like a simmering volcano. A president had been assassinated, the Civil Rights struggle was being met with increasing violence, and the war in Vietnam was escalating. Within the Black community the call for justice was rising in intensity and widening in scope; people tired of turning the other cheek were demanding the end of racism and challenging discrimination across the board. The demand for social change was stoking idealism, unleashing powerful emotions, and revealing the nation's violent undertow.

When she left Ghana Maya Angelou's future path seemed clear: she was returning to America to work with Malcolm X as the coordinator of his newly formed Organization of Afro-American Unity. After spending a few weeks in San Francisco with her family she planned to move to New York and go to work. To her delight her brother, Bailey, was waiting to greet her when she arrived in California. Her mother's home was as welcoming and lively as ever. And though Lady B. was less than enthusiastic about Maya's plan to work with Malcolm X, she was overjoyed to have her daughter back in the States.

Maya had been home only a few days, her bags barely unpacked, when the news flashed that Malcolm X was dead. He had been shot down in front of his family and supporters while just beginning to deliver a speech at the Audubon Ballroom in Harlem.

←Windshield

The stunned and

I was still in shock eyes. Malcolm's murder ~~and~~ had demoralized me. There seemed to be no center in the universe ~~and~~ the known edges of the world had ~~withdrawn~~ become dim and inscrutable.

~~I was further consumed~~ Guilt over leaving Guy in Africa ~~took~~ wrapped itself around ~~me~~ became a hair shirt around me which I could not dislodge. Would his newly found and desperately held on to manishness cause him ~~to~~ say or do something to irritate the Ghanian authorities. ~~Anxiety, guilt, terror, and pain~~ I had ~~brought~~ to Hawaii, and in the few months ~~that the~~ pestilence had abated to some degree. Friends in N.Y. informed ~~me that~~ Malcolm's widow, Betty, had given birth to healthy twins, and although his dream of an organization of African American unity would not be realized, his family was hale and his friends were true.

~~from~~ I heard from friends in Ghana that Guy had started behaving much better the moment I left. Often people in general and young people in particular need the responsibility of having to depend upon themselves for their lives. I did not know

So I was leaving Hawaii ~~and~~ a lighter and brighter person. ~~The~~ I knew I was going to Los Angeles. What I would do there and who I would find, but life was waiting on me and I knew it. ~~was~~

I got back on Friday and Malcolm was killed on Sunday [February 21, 1965]. I had talked to him the day before. On Sunday, a friend called and said, "Maya, why did you come back to this country? These people are crazy." And I said, "Yes, I know." She said, "Otherwise why would they have killed that man?" I hung up the phone, because I knew it was Malcolm and I couldn't speak.

—STEPHANIE CARUANA, "MAYA ANGELOU: AN INTERVIEW"

Her brother-friend and mentor was dead. Malcolm had told her about the death threats, but she'd convinced herself that no harm would come to him. The news of his murder devastated her. She has said that when deeply disturbed she becomes somewhat narcoleptic—sleep claims her, as it did on that Sunday morning. She aroused only to be further shocked and depressed in the days that followed by the seeming indifference of most of the Black folks around her.

She was adrift, no longer sure where to go or what to do, when Bailey came to her rescue. He convinced her to move to Hawaii, where he was then living, and resume her singing career. Bailey even arranged a nightclub booking for her. And it was her wise brother who predicted that the same people who were indifferent or hostile to Malcolm and took his murder so lightly would in a few short years become his champions.

Heartsick, needing time to grieve and heal and make sense out of the seeming madness of America, Maya moved to Hawaii and reluctantly began singing again. She was working at a club called the Encore, and despite not having sung professionally for several

(OPPOSITE) In an early draft of her memoir *A Song Flung Up to Heaven*, handwritten on a yellow legal pad, Maya recalls the troubled state of her spirit in the wake of Malcolm X's assassination. *(Angelou-Johnson Family Archives)*

years, she quickly regained her footing. But this time her heart wasn't in it. "I didn't care enough about my own singing to make other people appreciate it." The night she went to hear Della Reese sing at a rival club, Maya realized that she had to make a change:

> Listening to Della Reese, I knew that I would never call myself a singer again. . . . I would return to the mainland and search until I found something I loved doing. I might get a job as a waitress and try to finish a stage play I had begun in Accra. I had notebooks full of poems, maybe I'd try to finish them, polish them up, make them presentable and introduce them to a publisher and pray a lot.
>
> —MAYA ANGELOU, *A SONG FLUNG UP TO HEAVEN*

Her self-imposed exile in Hawaii had lasted for six months, but now it was time to move on. When she'd first decided to focus on writing Maya moved to New York to join the Harlem Writers Guild. Not this time. Malcolm had been murdered in Harlem and her emotions were still too raw. Instead of New York, Maya chose to settle in Los Angeles, the city she'd called home during the period when she briefly reigned as a calypso queen. She moved into a tiny apartment amidst a small community of friends. Her old friend Frances Williams, an actor and a well-connected political activist, had found her the space and was her neighbor. The extraordinary actor Beah Richards, one of the profession's grande dames, lived next door. Maya was writing, taking dance classes, renewing friendships, enjoying kitchen table woman talk with sister-friends, meet-

Della Reese was announced and when she ~~had~~ appeared there was an audible gasp. She was nearly six feet tall and very beautiful, and was ~~dressed~~ wearing what could be called a prom gown. There were no sequins or beads or shiny stars on her dress. She was certainly not ~~dressed up~~ costumed for show business. After a short introduction she started to sing and I understood why the regulars at my cafe had left in record numbers.

Della had a huge voice, which she could modulate to a whisper, and her ear was perfect. She ~~could~~ could send her tone to the foundation of the earth then lift it to glimmer in the air like the sound of pinched crystal.

ing a few men and flirting a bit. And to make ends meet, she was working part-time as a market researcher going door-to-door in Watts interviewing women about the products they used.

Those questions seemed particularly ironic given that the community was being gouged by high prices, but lacked goods and services. Once a vibrant working-class community, Watts had fallen on hard times. It was being racked by unemployment, schools were decaying, family bonds were fraying, and a rootless generation of young people was beginning to vent their frustration and anger. She had been working there for several weeks—listening to women talk about their lives, noting the profound changes in the community, the simmering despair and rage—when Watts exploded on August 11, 1965.

Maya with her brother, Bailey, and a woman friend in 1965 in Hawaii, where for a brief period Maya went back to singing professionally. *(Angelou-Johnson Family Archives)*

Unable to simply sit and watch it on television, Maya went back into the community. While canvassing she'd noted the gathering storm, now despite the threat of arrest or worse, she felt compelled to bear witness: "On the first day of the insurgency, people of all ages allowed their rage to drive them to the streets. But on the fourth day, the anger of the old was spent. I read sadness and even futility on their faces. But I saw no attempt to dissuade the younger rioters from their hurly-burly behavior" (Angelou, *A Song Flung Up to Heaven*).

Watts flamed for six days, 34 people were killed, over 1,000 were injured, and nearly 4,000 arrested. It was the first of what would become a series of urban uprisings. Years later, when asked a question about racism, Maya would aptly sum up the causes of the "Watts Rebellion" as she always refers to it:

> When the human race neglects its weaker members, when the family neglects its weakest one—it's the first blow in a suicidal movement. I see the neglect in cities around the country, in poor white children in West Virginia and Virginia and Kentucky—in the big cities, too, for that matter. I see the neglect of Native American children in the concentration camps called reservations.
>
> The powerful say, "Pull yourself up by your bootstraps." But they don't really believe that those living on denuded reservations, or on strip-mined hills, or in ghettos that are destinations for drugs from Colombia and Iraq, can somehow pull themselves up. What they're really saying is, "If you can, do, but if you can't, forget it." It's the most pernicious of all acts of segregation, because it is so subtle.
>
> —KEN KELLY, "VISIONS: MAYA ANGELOU," *MOTHER JONES*, MAY/JUNE 1995

Black America was crying out and raging in the streets. There were stories that needed to be told, truths calling to be spoken. Maya

When Maya returned from Ghana in 1965 she planned to settle in New York City and work with Malcolm X, but in the wake of his assassination she took refuge in Hawaii and later Los Angeles. By the late 1960s she was finally back in New York, the town she loved, writing full-time and attending parties like this one. *(Angelou-Johnson Family Archives)*

Angelou wanted to bring them to the stage as a playwright and into print as a poet.

She had joined the actor Frank Silvera's theater company, the Theatre of Being, and was once again appearing on stage, more by fluke than design. Her neighbor and friend Beah Richards was to star in his production of *Medea* but she didn't drive and needed a way to get back and forth. Maya, whose job as a market researcher had gone up in flames, volunteered to be her chauffeur and ended up auditioning for the role of the Nurse. She won the part but received no direction on her character or performance. Silvera's attentions were totally on Beah Richards. To Maya's surprise, the critics made note of her performance, though not her name since she wasn't listed in the program. But she hungered to be the playwright, not the actor, and by 1966 was growing increasingly more restive in Los Angeles.

She had written *All Day Long*, a play that focused on one day in the life of a Black boy from the South struggling to adjust to living in a northern city. When she asked Silvera for advice he offered little more than a crumb: "Find a producer." She went to the library, researched the process and searched in vain for someone to back her play, which she admits was "a slight piece."

By the time her friend Rosa Guy arrived in L.A. to promote her book *Bird at My Window*, Maya had decided that L.A. was not the place for her. In Rosa's company Maya's best memories of New York came rushing forward. The city once again called her name.

She had a place to stay; Rosa had offered to share her large apartment. Maya was in the midst of planning her departure when her brother arrived at her door bearing grim news. Guy had been hit by a truck in San Francisco and was in the hospital, his condition serious. His schooling finished, Guy had arrived at his grandmother's home only three days before from Ghana. His homecoming was to have been a surprise for Maya, instead it was a nightmare revisited.

Rosa Guy was still visiting when Bailey came with the news. Maya, her brother, and Rosa piled into the car. All Maya wanted to do was curl up and retreat into sleep, but her brother was too exhausted to take the wheel, so Maya drove all the way north, a seven-hour journey, her worry increasing with each passing mile.

Her mother was waiting for her when she arrived at the hospital. It was Lady B. who told her that her son's neck had once again been broken, but that the prognosis was good. When she walked into his room her heart eased when she saw that her son was awake and alert. And unlike the lonely vigil she'd maintained in Ghana, this time she had her mother and brother beside her. The doctors assured Maya that Guy would recover, as did he, during the days she spent at his bedside watching him heal, listening to his plans, marveling at the man he'd

Maya met her sister-writer, the novelist Rosa Guy, when she moved to New York and joined the Harlem Writers Guild. Their close friendship spans nearly fifty years. (*Angelou-Johnson Family Archives*)

become. Guy was well on the road to recovery when Maya returned to Los Angeles. "I left San Francisco when I saw Guy sitting up like a golden prince and being served like a king in my mother's house" (Angelou, *A Song Flung Up to Heaven*).

She spent several more months in L.A. working to build a nest egg, spending time with and saying farewell to friends and family before heading east. Finally, nearly two years after her return to America, she was back in the city that had been her original destination when she left Ghana. Buoyed by New York's energy and the presence of friends, back in the fold of the Writers Guild, Maya blossomed and hunkered down to concentrate on her work.

Chief among those cheering her on was her "brother" James Baldwin. Maya first met him in Paris while on tour with *Porgy and Bess* and they'd been close friends ever since. They were kindred spirits in so many ways, both brilliant intellectuals with quick wits and amazing memories, who shared a profound respect for words written and spoken, and great hope for and love of their people. To Maya, James was

> a whirlwind who stirred everything and everybody. He lived at a dizzying pace and I loved spinning with him. Once after we had spent an afternoon talking and drinking with a group of White writers in a downtown bar, he said he liked that I could hold my liquor and my positions. He was pleased that I could defend Edgar Allan Poe and ask serious questions about Willa Cather.
>
> —ANGELOU, *A SONG FLUNG UP TO HEAVEN*

The two shared a passion for social justice, for owning their lives, and speaking their truths, regardless of what others might think. Like her beloved brother, Bailey, Jimmy Baldwin was physically much shorter than Maya and totally fearless, and he too considered himself very much her "big" brother protector and champion. New York was his hometown and he immediately took her into the bosom of his family, and his mother and siblings claimed her as one of their clan.

She found a brother in Jimmy Baldwin and a true sister in Dolly McPherson. Maya and Dolly discovered that they were both being wooed by the same wealthy, powerful Ghanaian, but instead of squaring off as rivals, they became lifelong friends. Dolly, who was a program officer with the Institute of International Education, had previously taught English at Lincoln University in Missouri. The two shared a passion for literature and libraries and scholarship, and a mutual admiration for each other's intelligence and common sense. They loved laughter, wonderful parties, good food, and both knew a thing or two about men. Dolly, who was originally from New Orleans, and Maya shared a similar sensibility about the importance of family, friendship, hospitality, and grace. And, like Maya's mother, they were women who could be both tough and tender as well as fierce in their loyalties and in defense of those they loved.

Maya was once again surrounded by friends and chosen family, all encouraging her writing. She had found an apartment just off Central Park on the Upper West Side of Manhattan and decorated it on a shoestring and with beautiful furnishings given by friends. Her struggle to write and earn a living had been immeasurably eased by the generosity of another friend, Jerry Purcell, who supported her writing by providing a stipend. They had become friends when Maya sang at his supper club and Purcell, a successful entrepreneur, had branched out into talent management. "Purcell treated me like a valued employee. Save for the odd temporary office job and the money I made writing radio spots for Ruby Dee and Ossie Davis, I depended upon his largesse. He didn't once ask for anything and seemed totally satisfied with a simple thanks" (Angelou, *A Song Flung Up to Heaven*).

By the spring of 1968 Maya was busily writing: She'd completed two plays since returning to New York, a drama, *The Clawing Within*, and a two-act musical with an African theme she'd titled *Adjoa Amissa*, and she was working on a group of poems about being Black and female. But when Martin Luther King Jr. asked her to join his upcoming Poor People's March on Washington, D.C., she couldn't refuse. Having agreed to spend a month on the road eliciting the support of Black preachers and raising money, Maya was

On the terrace: Maya and her sister-friend Rosa Guy and a male friend enjoying the breeze in the summer of 1968. *(Angelou-Johnson Family Archives)*

slated to begin after her birthday on April 4. The morning of her birthday, in the midst of preparing for the party she was hosting to celebrate her fortieth year, Maya heard the news that Martin had been murdered.

She had agreed to work with King again, because she had seen

While in the Bay Area working on the series *Blacks, Blues, Black!* that she wrote for public television in 1968, Maya, her brother, Bailey, at her side (right), posed with a group of children in Oakland, California. *(Angelou-Johnson Family Archives)*

him grow, "broadening his sight to include all oppressed people." Like Malcolm, he too had embarked on a more radical transformative mission. In her later years she would describe these two giants as being "like peaches and cream." Three years earlier she'd returned to America to work with Malcolm and he'd been murdered and in a macabre twist of fate she had been poised to join Martin when he too was assassinated. Once again she shut down, dulled by grief. This time it was her brother Jimmy Baldwin who pulled her out of her shell, urging her to write, reminding her that she was strong and resilient, sharing her pain and encouraging her laughter.

If 1968 was a year of great pain, loss, and sadness, it was also the year when America first witnessed the breadth and depth of Maya Angelou's spirit and creative genius. Out of the blue she received an invitation to write a ten-part series on African American culture for the San Francisco affiliate of the Public Broadcasting System (PBS), then called National Education Television (NET). Enrico Banducci, the owner of the hungry i, a nightclub in San Francisco and a friend from the days she'd sung calypso, had recommended her for the project. It was an incredible opportunity. Especially given the fact that other than the short essays she'd written for her friends Ruby Dee and Ossie Davis's radio show and a story that had been published in a Cuban magazine, Maya hadn't sold any of her work in the

United States and had never written for television. But when asked if she was interested, Maya Angelou immediately said yes.

Anyone who courts success should also be willing to risk failure. This wasn't the first time that Maya Angelou dared to step up to a new challenge, and it wouldn't be the last. She'd taught herself at fifteen years old to drive on a dusty Mexican road in the middle of the night; broken the color line to become a cable car conductor; transformed herself into a calypso queen; bluffed her way into a career as a journalist in Cairo. When the offer came to write the television series Maya buried herself in the library. "If you ask for something you have to be prepared to accept it. I spent days in the library. I was the first to arrive and the last to leave, poring over books about television documentaires. I read everything that I could lay my hands on about writing, producing, and directing television documentaries. While still in the midst of my self-designed crash course, I began writing the series" (as told to Marcia Ann Gillespie).

A promotional piece for the acclaimed series *Blacks, Blues, Black!* that Maya created for KQED, San Francisco's public television station. *(Courtesy KQED)*

BLACKS, BLUES, BLACK!
with MAYA ANGELOU
writer, producer, hostess in a ten-week series

beginning monday, july 8 at 8 pm
kqed channel 9

The series Maya created, *Blacks, Blues, Black!*, explored the interrelationships between African and African American culture and the powerful influence of Africa on Western culture. In addition to writing, Maya also narrated the series, which was filmed in San Francisco, and was involved in directing and producing it as well. She highlighted the musical connections from traditional African drumming and chants to worksongs, the blues, jazz, and gospel. She demonstrated the many ways Africa influenced social and modern dance and the modern artists of the West. The series featured powerful performances by a wide range of singers, dancers, and musicians and got great reviews when it aired in 1968. It became a staple on NET and its successor, PBS, for many years.

Maya Angelou was reaching for her dream.

Robert Loomis, an editor at Random House, had called her just as she was beginning work on *Blacks, Blues, Black!* He asked if she was interested in writing her autobiography. She didn't think she'd lived long enough to consider telling her story, and more to the point, she wanted to publish poetry, to write and direct plays. She said no, but Loomis persisted, and finally, just as she was winding up the series and preparing to return to New York, he called again and this time knew exactly how to get the answer he was seeking. "I'm sure he talked to [James] Baldwin because he . . . called and said, 'Miss Angelou, it's been nice talking to you. I'm rather glad that you decided not to write an autobiography because to write an autobiography as literature is the most difficult thing anyone can do.' I said, 'I'll do it' " (Claudia Tate, ed., *Black Women Writers at Work*, Continuum, 1983).

She began to work on the book, putting her initial thoughts on paper while sitting in her mother's kitchen in California, thoughts about the human spirit and what it takes for us to rise in the face of adversity and a line from a poem she'd learned as a child:

What you looking at me for?
I didn't come to stay . . .

She had found the opening for her book. "Nothing so frightens me as writing, but nothing so satisfies me. It's like a swimmer in the [English] Channel: you face the stingrays and waves and cold and grease, and finally you reach the other shore, and you put your foot on the ground—Aaaaahhhhh!" (Lawrence Toppman, "Maya Angelou: The Serene Spirit of a Survivor," Charlotte *Observer,* 1983).

During the months she spent writing the book, Maya practically withdrew from the world. She'd set the bar high. Her ambition was to write a book that would be more than her story. It would speak to and honor the Black experience and affirm the "human spirit." She more than achieved her goal. She wrote a coming-of-age story that has become a modern classic.

When *I Know Why the Caged Bird Sings* was published in 1970 it immediately became a bestseller. Readers, especially women, and in particular Black women, took the book to heart, felt affirmed by its message, shared it with friends and family, and were eager to meet and embrace the writer, to hear her speak, to learn more from and about her. Nominated for a National Book Award, never out of print, published in a range of languages, available worldwide, *Caged Bird* is assigned reading in countless schools and universities, studied by writers and scholars, and lovingly passed on by one generation of readers to the next.

Maya Angelou became an autobiographer because she couldn't turn away from a challenge, but poetry was in her blood. She'd fallen in love with poetry in Stamps, Arkansas. Her favorite poems

were indelibly imprinted in her memory and she assiduously studied the poetry and the poets she admired. For years she studied the form, haunting libraries, reading widely, constantly writing and rewriting, polishing and perfecting her own poems. Her goal had long been to see her poetry published and, even in the midst of writing her autobiography, Maya the poet was still at work. The year before the publication of *Caged Bird*, she took a giant step toward achieving her goal when she recorded *The Poetry of Maya Angelou* (GWP records). When her first collection of poetry, *Just Give Me a Cool Drink of Water 'Fore I Diiie*, followed in 1971 it became a bestseller and was nominated for a Pulitzer Prize. These powerfully evocative poems gave voice to the Black woman's experience in America and the experience of being woman and human. Each word carefully chosen, complex rhythms distilled, meanings layered, her poems reflect the richness and subtlety of Black speech and sensibilities in the hands of a master; each poem crying to be read aloud.

It was poetry that helped Maya Angelou trust her voice again when she was a mute hurting child. Mrs. Flowers, the woman who'd been the first to nurture Maya's intellect, had told her

"Poetry is music written for the human voice. Until you read it aloud you will never love it." So when I was about twelve, I went under the house and started to speak poetry. Until I felt it over my tongue, through my teeth and across my lips, I would never love it. That has influenced the way I hear poetry when I'm writing it; I write for the voice, not the eye.

—TOPPMAN, "MAYA ANGELOU: THE SERENE SPIRIT OF A SURVIVOR"

BLAZING NEW

TRAILS

A IS FOR AFRICA

CHOSEN PLACE TIMELESS PEOPLE

HARLEM
LIBERTY
HOUSE
PROUDLY PRESENTS
BLACK
WOMEN
WRITERS
Maya Angelou
Jeanne Bond
Rosa Guy
Paule Marshall

SOUL CLAP HANDS AND SING

BIRD AT MY WINDOW

I KNOW WHY THE CAGE BIRD SINGS

BROWN GIRL, BROWN STONES

I KNOW WHY THE CAGE BIRD SINGS

BIRD AT MY WINDOW

CHOSEN PLACE TIMELESS PEOPLE

A IS FOR AFRICA

READING,

LAUGHING,

LOVING,

COMMUNICATING

SUNDAY, APRIL 26th, 1970   at 5p.m.   129th & 7th   Admission 99¢

SOUL CLAP HANDS AND SING

BROWN GIRL, BROWN STONES

Flyer advertising a reading by Maya and three of her sister-writers in New York City in 1970.

Black America was brimming with a renewed sense of pride and purpose: People calling for Black Power, announcing to the world, I'm Black, and I'm Proud, celebrating their culture and creativity. The Black Arts movement was in its ascendancy; playwrights and poets were in the vanguard of the cultural explosion. Black theater companies were springing up in cities both large and small across the country, the works of Black playwrights were attracting critical attention and filling theaters. Readings by Black poets were being held in bars and churches and auditoriums and concert halls. Folks lined up to hear Sonia Sanchez, Nikki Giovanni, Jayne Cortez, and Maya Angelou.

Some people might choose to lay back and coast and enjoy the attention, but Maya Angelou is a swimmer in constant motion, moving from one body of water to another. Her first goal had been to become a playwright; she'd already written several plays but had yet to see one produced. Her work on *Blacks, Blues, Black!* further fueled her desire not only to write, but also to direct film, no matter that Hollywood remained resistant to Blacks and women in those roles.

She wrote a script, *Georgia, Georgia,* in 1971, which told the story of a love affair between two American expatriates, an African

American singer and a White American photographer. To her initial delight, Cinerama, a Swedish film company, bought it, but then the producers declined to consider Maya as director. The film, which starred the superb actor, Diana Sands, was shot in 1972 in Sweden with Swedish director, Stig Björkman. It was a bittersweet experience for Maya. There she was on the set watching a man who had no real understanding of Black culture or people, no feeling for the nuances of the experience, direct the film. She had also composed the score for the film but was being stonewalled in her attempts to work with the music director. And instead of offering camaraderie, the cast, perhaps taking their cues from the director, kept their distance.

Demoralized, and beginning to doubt herself, she reached out to her mother. Vivian Baxter immediately sprang into action. She jumped on a plane and flew to Stockholm to bolster her daughter's flagging spirits.

In an interview more than a decade later, Maya recalled her mother's pep talk:

> "Baby, mother came to Stockholm to tell you one thing—a cow needs a tail for more than one season. . . . Well, the cow that thinks because summer is over it can drop its least needed and most laughed at part and stomp on it, is a fool. Because if it lives, spring will come and the flies will be back and it will want nothing so much as that very tail. You do your work. If they live, they will be back to you."
>
> —JUDITH PATERSON, "INTERVIEW: MAYA ANGELOU,"
> *VOGUE*, SEPTEMBER 1982

(ABOVE) Maya Angelou and Paul Du Feu met in London, married in San Francisco in 1974, and settled for a while in Sonoma, California. Here the two share kitchen duties. *(Photo by Ron Groeper)*

(OPPOSITE) An early draft of the lyrics for "So It Goes!" a song Maya wrote for Roberta Flack.

Rather than retreating and licking her wounds after *Georgia, Georgia,* the experience stiffened her resolve. Her mother's advice to, "Just do your work!" became her mantra. But Maya was equally determined never to allow the work to consume her life. There was always time for family and friends, for parties with music and dancing, good food, talk and laughter, and most especially for love. And during a stay in England in 1972 Maya was smitten when a tall Welshman named Paul Du Feu came up to her at a party and told her that she "was the most beautiful woman in the world."

The two quickly became a hot item. "He courted me in London, before I was published there. We were in a wine bar in the King's Road and an American who knew me came up and said to him, 'Do you realize this is one of the heaviest women in America . . . how are you going to cope?' And Paul turned and said, 'I am a weight lifter.' And I thought oooooooh" (Bev Gilligan, "How Maya Angelou Overcame All the Odds" *Woman,* October 1987).

When the couple married in 1973, it caused a stir in some quarters: Some people took umbrage because Du Feu, the former husband of the noted feminist author Germaine Greer, was White. Others raised eyebrows because he was a few years younger than she and had posed nude for the British *Playgirl* magazine, or because he was a carpenter and homebuilder and a minor writer. In countless

So it Goes

We ran into her just by chance
I saw it in a single glance
My oldest friend   your new romance.

And I learned that

Love is a rush of wild wind
The scent of a summer rose
A whistle blowing on a distant track
And when it goes — it goes
So it Goes

You couldn't run, she couldn't hide
She dropped her eyes, you turned aside
You didn't want to hurt my pride

But you knew that

I like you best when your heart was free

Now Take your heart to the place it
where it longs to be

I don't want to bind you to a memory
I know if I wait love will happen to me

interviews Maya was often asked to respond to the criticisms, but refused to be baited. Years later, when asked about love and marriage she would say, "If you have enough courage to love someone, and also if you have the unmitigated gall to accept love in return, then you are an inspiration to the species."

After marrying in San Francisco, the couple decided to settle in California. With her new husband cheering her on, Maya's work moved into high gear. Determined to become a director, she returned to Sweden and enrolled in film school to hone her skills and in 1974 enrolled at the American Film Institute in Los Angeles, where for her class project she returned to a play she'd written nearly a decade before. She rewrote and produced *All Day Long* as a short film.

While studying at the institute, Maya's second autobiography, *Gather Together in My Name,* was published. This book detailed her struggles as a young single mother as she stumbled and nearly succumbed to the fast hard life, nearly lost her son, and nearly lost herself. During this same period she also wrote an adaptation of Sophocles' *Ajax* and saw the two-act play brought to life on the stage of the prestigious Mark Taper Forum in Los Angeles. Her mother had told her to "Just do your work!" and she was doing that and more.

May 9, 1975

Dear Mom,

As Mother's Day approaches, in fact as every day
approaches, I think of you with such joy and
gratitude and laughter. I hope the Mediterranean
is pretty and blue and warm and pleasing you.
If there is any fun in any port, I'm certain
that you will find it and use it and remember
every detail of it so that when you return to
the warm, waiting, welcoming arms of your family
you can report every incident. I trust that the
passengers on your ship are pleasant and not too
demanding and that your shipboard romances are
all handsome and generous and plentiful.

Now, as for Sonoma and Stockton, your family
(grandson, granddaughter, sone-in-law and daughter)
are getting along as well as we can be expected to in
your absence. Our health remains top form and spirits
are fine. We're all pleased with our work, in fact,
we're swingin' - except, of course, our mother figure
is ballin' somewhere thousands and thousands of miles
away. We are reassured because we know between,
during and after drinks and laughs and dancing and
working she thinks of us.

We love you dearly and miss you, Mom.

                    S'agapo,

She was writing at a feverish pace, a yellow note-pad never far from her hand. Constantly testing new waters, stretching as an artist, taking risks: poet and lecturer, autobiographer and screenwriter, activist, student and scholar. She'd been invited to teach and had been named a visiting professor by several colleges and universities and received the first of what would become a veritable shower of honorary degrees. And in the midst of it all Maya Angelou, the actor, somewhat reluctantly, stepped back into the spotlight.

"Anytime I've acted I've been twisted into it." When Broadway beckoned in 1973, she accepted the role in *Look Away* because she wanted her costar, Geraldine Page, to perform in one of her plays.

Look Away explored the relationship between Mary Todd Lincoln, Abraham Lincoln's widow, and her confidante, Mrs. Elizabeth Keckley, who made the First Lady's dresses. A former slave who became a renowned dressmaker, Keckley had written about her relationship with Lincoln in her memoir, *Behind the Scenes, or Thirty Years a Slave and Four Years in the White House*. The two-character play, directed by Page's husband, Rip Torn, closed immediately after its official opening. But Maya, who had immersed herself in Keckley's life in preparation for the role, was nominated for a Tony Award for her performance.

As an actor she had consistently attracted good notices from the critics, and if acting had been her passion the Tony nomination would surely have been a powerful incentive to pull out all the stops. But Maya would remain a reluctant actor, taking only the occasional role, usually at the urging of friends or with some other goal in mind.

When her friend Alex Haley's landmark book *Roots* was slated to be filmed as a mini-series for television, Maya, who wanted to direct two segments agreed to play Ngo Buto, the grandmother of the epic's hero, Kunta Kinte. The film version of Haley's multigenerational family epic was an extraordinary event. It aired in 1977 and was watched by millions of Americans who seemed to make a visceral connection to the African American experience—the nightmare of slavery and the great march to freedom—through this

Maya and Alex Haley, her dear friend and author of *Roots*, in California in 1971. *(Angelou-Johnson Family Archives)*

family saga. Maya received an Emmy nomination for her performance, one of the many powerful performances singled out for awards, and captured widespread public attention. In 1976, the year before *Roots* aired, Maya's third autobiography, *Singin' and Swingin' and Gettin' Merry Like Christmas*, chronicling her first marriage, the somewhat serendipitous road to becoming an actor and successful nightclub performer, and her budding dream to write, had been published. Her second book of poetry, *Oh Pray My Wings Are Gonna Fit Me Well*, a collection honoring the sacrifice and struggle of our Black ancestors, was also in print. She'd written two television specials, *The Legacy* and *The Inheritors*; seen one of her plays, *And Still I Rise*, produced; and been named a Woman of the Year by the

He smiled and the muscles ~~in his~~
~~Every muscle moved~~ ~~in a~~ rippled in
his face like water falling over a
washboard. He moved and his
arms and legs floated with ~~oiled~~ and
what seemed to be oiled precision
His teeth were white and even as new
tombstones and he ~~liked me~~ had an
extraordinary apetite for Louisiana
food, for he came to the New Orleans
Cafe where I worked at least once
a day. In the way that women and
men have always known when they
had caught the fancy of member
the opposite sex I knew he liked
me and even wanted me, when he entered the door, I flew
to him

Ladies' Home Journal, one of the nation's premier women's magazines. But as a result of the phenomenal success of *Roots,* which set a record for the number of television viewers when it aired, Maya became better known to the public as an actor rather than as a writer. As she recounted in an interview given in the midst of *Roots* fever: "I found that people knew me. . . . I've written five books, I can't say how many plays, movie scripts, music, and poetry and so forth. I walk down the street and people say, 'You're the actress in Roots. What's your name again, and what have you been doing all this time?' " (Curt Davis, "Maya Angelou: And Still She Rises," *Encore,* September 1977).

She had been doing her work.

(OPPOSITE) Maya writing about a former lover in an early draft of *Gather Together in My Name.*

For a 3 day in ~~for the~~ the spring
1. Cicely and I had ~~spent 3~~
~~days in Savanna Geo.,~~ worked
together in Sa. Ga. as members of
the cast of Al Haley "Roots". ~~She~~
Although she had played ——
the mother and I had acted
the role of Nyo Boto, the grandmother.
I had no illusion that their
was any inequity in our real
life roles. She was a serious
and busy working woman and
so was I.
2. Her mother had been fierce
in dictating Cicely's rehearsal ~~time~~, schedule
and performing schedule. ~~She~~
'I decided when I could dictate my
own life, I would never touch another

(Notes for article on Cicely Tyson)
Piano. I realize that was youthful
rebellion. Now I ~~feel~~ know I'm moving
closer to my own maturity.
I might play again. I might.
Maybe.   Notes
3. ~~some~~ I sublimate. I take
the passion and put it totally
into the passion of the character.
It always works.
4 - remove typos
5 ——
6 - answer
7 ——
8 —— The relationship lasted
three years.
9 - She now lives alone ~~on house~~ really
on Sg Calif. "I need the sound of the
sea. Funny huh. I was born in New York
City, in the heart of Harlem. But when
I heard the roar of the Ocean I

" . . . . Sometimes I know that I am involved in a lifelong search. And I even know what I am searching for." She hesitates, living in a quiet moment, then her hands begin to fly around in the air like two dark birds frightened out of their nest. "And at other times I not only don't know what I'm ~~going to~~ searching for, but I ~~even have difficulty~~ Why I'm ~~have doubts~~ understanding the ~~search at all~~." She laughs. ~~The~~ Reddened lips stretch across ~~to~~ large white teeth that protrude just enough to make her smile distinctive. Cicely Tyson is considered one of the great American Beauties. Her picture looks out of the Nations slick paged

Magazine, surrounded by the photographs of Faye Dunaway and Ali McGraw and other current ~~though White~~ American Beauties. Yet if her large white teeth protruded one more millimeter she would lose her place in a beauty contest because ~~by default of~~ an over bite.

Maya's notes on an article she was writing about one of her dearest friends, the actress Cicely Tyson, for *Redbook* magazine.

Maya dancing poolside at her home in Sonoma, California, in 1974. *(Angelou–Johnson Family Archives)*

CHAPTER 6

Doing Her Work

I believe that the force that created life is
betting that human beings will do something quite
wonderful—like live up to their potential.

—MAYA ANGELOU (1989)

for a few month I was a novelty
then the attendance began to wane
I was told that people had come
other club to listen to a real singer
riosity led me. Then came a ...
en there was a decided drop. Au
eness. Night after night attenda
egan to wane until it became
mmon to find the club only a t
ll at showtime I was told tha
rival. I had hired an
thentic singer. I went alone to
to see my competitor and the
t spot the show made me come to
grips with my life.

Della Reese was announced an
hen she appeared there was an
dible gasp. She was nearly six feet
ll and very beautiful and wat
aring what could be called a gro
own. There were no sequins or bea
f phony stars on her dress. She was
tainly not dressed in costume for

WHEN MAYA ANGELOU CELEBRATED HER FIFTIETH BIRTHDAY on April 4, 1978, she could look back on a decade of great work and reward. She had accomplished more than many artists hope to achieve in a lifetime: There were five books in print, all bestsellers. Two had been nominated for prestigious awards (the Pulitzer Prize and the National Book Award). A third collection of poetry, *And Still I Rise*, was due out that year. She was the first African American woman to have a screenplay (*Georgia, Georgia*) produced. Several of her plays had been staged. She was an accomplished, highly regarded, though somewhat reluctant actor who had received Tony and Emmy nominations for her work. She'd narrated, produced, and directed a number of projects for PBS and won their Golden Eagle Award for her documentary series, *Afro-Americans in the Arts*. Her work was recognized and acclaimed internationally, especially in the United Kingdom, where she was a much sought after speaker, frequently interviewed and profiled on television and by the press. She maintained a whirlwind schedule—writing, directing, lecturing, and teaching at colleges and universities, serving on numerous distinguished panels and commissions, and in constant demand as a public speaker. She was being showered with awards and honorary degrees.

Her personal life was also blossoming, with family and a constantly expanding circle of friends proudly supportive of her

At a meeting at Occidental College, Maya and three of her dearest friends—James Baldwin, Roscoe Lee Browne, and M. J. (Mary Jane) Hewitt—share a light moment reminiscing about their brother Godfrey Cambridge prior to attending his funeral in Los Angeles in 1976. *(Angelou-Johnson Family Archives)*

accomplishments, sharing laughter, cheering her on. She was celebrating her fifth wedding anniversary. She and Paul seemed happily paired, each busy in their chosen careers, each proud of the other's talents and accomplishments, playful and easy together. When Maya, an amazing cook was in the kitchen, Paul would often be at her side doing prep work, pouring drinks, telling jokes, making her laugh. But by the end of the decade, the couple had drifted apart, the marriage once so vibrant had withered and the two officially parted ways in 1981.

In an interview several years later, Maya reflected on the breakup: "As the fame and the success increased and the books were bestsellers, and I became the first Black producer in Hollywood, he couldn't stand it. . . . I brought all my energy and laughter and frivolity and seriousness to the marriage and it failed. It wore out. I don't think I failed. It failed" (Bev Gilligan, "How Maya Angelou Overcame All the Odds," *Woman*, 1987).

Just as her marriage had worn out, so too was her patience with Hollywood wearing thin. Although she'd written, produced, and directed a number of television documentaries and small film projects, she'd yet to receive a green light to direct a major project. And as had happened in Sweden years before with *Georgia, Georgia,*

The writer at work.
Maya literally puts pen
to paper, always on
yellow legal pads, and
keeps a deck of cards
close by, sometimes
a crossword as well,
to occupy her "little
mind," she says, while
she's working through
a writing challenge.
*(Photo by Wayne
Miller, Magnum
Photos)*

Maya was often forced to watch her screenplays handed over to White male directors. She had been primarily responsible for writing the screenplay for the TV film version of her autobiography, *I Know Why the Caged Bird Sings*, but was excluded from many of the artistic decisions. The resulting film was a pale imitation of the original work.

Breaking new ground. Maya on location in Sweden, where her screenplay, *Georgia, Georgia* was being filmed. Stig Björkman, the director, is at right. *(Photo copyright © 1972 Cinerama Releasing)*

Still, when Twentieth Century-Fox hired her as a producer in 1979, the same year *Caged Bird* aired, she had high hopes. She wrote a script, *Sister, Sister*, exploring the flaring tensions in a middle-class Black southern family when three sisters are reunited at their father's funeral. It was to be the pilot for a television series. But her dreams of directing the film were dashed when studio executives insisted on a "bankable" White male director. (The casting, however, was superb: Diahann Carroll, Rosalind Cash, and Irene Cara played the three sisters, with Paul Winfield and Robert Hooks in key roles.) More disappointment followed when the studio shelved the film after it was made and canceled all plans for the series.

Sister, Sister languished for several years before finally being aired in 1982, but by then Maya Angelou had already packed her bags and moved on. Some people were surprised when they heard the news that she'd relocated to Winston-Salem, North Carolina. They shouldn't have been. It was a homecoming of sorts for the woman who spent her childhood in Stamps, Arkansas, in her paternal grandmother's wise keeping. Her Black southern roots informed her sense of faith and civility. And the South was changing, had changed dramatically. Though the struggle was far from done, African Americans were claiming ground. A reverse migration was beginning, and Maya's move became a symbol for many that one could go home again.

Winston-Salem was no southern backwater. A small verdant city it boasts several highly rated colleges and universities, a vibrant arts community, and, thanks to the Moravians who founded Salem, more liberal leanings. When Maya accepted the appointment as a Reynolds Professor of American Studies at Wake Forest University she saw it both as an opportunity to stretch her wings as a teacher and as an opportune place to write. "I've taken the chair for one semester a year until 1985, so that gives me the spring and summer to write" (interview with Judith Patterson, *Vogue,* 1982).

But she was also much taken by Winston-Salem's lush terrain and gracious people, and Maya was quick to say how much she loved teaching at Wake Forest. That love affair was mutual, so much so that in a break from tradition, the university made hers a lifetime position. It was a singular honor, in the past the Reynolds professorship had been a two- to five-year appointment.

The endowed chair afforded Maya free rein to teach any subject of her choosing in the humanities. The interpretation of poetry has often been her subject of choice, but her courses reflect her wide-

(THIS PAGE CLOCKWISE)
Maya with a few of her
many extraordinary
friends: Romare Bearden
*(photo © Susan Mullally
2006)*; Harry Belafonte
*(Angelou-Johnson Family
Archives)*; Roberta Flack
and Max Roach *(photo by
Ron Eckstein, 1987)*;

(OPPOSITE PAGE CLOCK-
WISE) Charles Kuralt
*(Angelou-Johnson Family
Archives)*; Andrew Young
and Jesse Jackson *(photo by
Al Price)*; James Baldwin
*(Angelou-Johnson Family
Archives)*; and Ray Charles
*(Angelou-Johnson Family
Archives)*

ranging interests—philosophy and ethics, history and social change, matters of race and identity, theology and science, theater and narrative writing.

> I have brilliant students. Brilliant. I'm a very hard teacher. I am a very good teacher. I use any ploy; do anything to convey my message. I will sing. I will read Shakespeare. They must read. They must debate.
>
> What I really teach is one thing: that is, I am a human being. Nothing human can be alien to me. That's all I teach.
>
> —AS TOLD TO MARCIA ANN GILLESPIE

From the moment she arrived on campus, students vied for the opportunity to sit in her classroom. It's considered an honor to be accepted in her class and enrollment is limited. For many years the course terminated with a staged public performance by the class that Maya produced and directed. In 1988 it became a full-scale theatrical event. The class performed Shakespeare's *Macbeth*, and Maya challenged herself and her audience by staging it with two casts, one all female and the other based on conventional male casting, in alternating performances.

When Maya moved to Winston-Salem in 1981, the city rolled out the red carpet, and she eagerly embraced the life of the community. Her sister-friend Dolly McPherson had also accepted a teaching position at Wake Forest and was living nearby, and Maya soon found other kindred spirits and her home became a gathering place for friends from far and near.

Maya often laughingly says that had her life taken a different turn she might have become a real estate agent. More likely a real estate mogul. She has a shrewd eye when it comes to picking homes and whether in California or North Carolina, she tends to favor large, roomy places. Her first home in Winston-Salem was no exception, and within a short time she was busily hiring contractors, adding and expanding rooms: extra bedrooms to accommodate her family and many friends; a glass-enclosed expanded dining room for the large dinner parties she regularly hosted; a large welcoming kitchen.

Ever the gracious hostess, Maya, wearing traditional Senegalese dress, in conversation with her guests and demonstrating her prowess as a chef as she prepares an African feast for her party, in a feature for *Bon Appétit* magazine in 1978. *(Photographed by Brian Leatart)*

There was a basketball court on the grounds where neighborhood children were allowed to play after politely asking her permission. But that court also symbolized her hope that one day she would see her grandson out there, ball in hand.

While Maya was still living in California, Guy, who was living in the Oakland–Bay Area, had been engaged in a long-term relationship with a woman and fathered a son they named Colin Ashanti. The relationship ended acrimoniously. There had been a bitter custody suit. Guy won, but in 1981 when Colin was two years old his mother took him and disappeared. Maya and Guy spent years and many thousands of dollars searching for him. Maya hired a team of private investigators who followed every lead no matter how slim. Though she never doubted that Colin would be returned to them, it would be eight long years before he was found and returned to his father.

A joyous Maya with her mother, Vivian; son, Guy; and grandson, Colin. *(Angelou-Johnson Family Archives)*

Faith, family, friendships, and work helped her get through that difficult period. In Winston-Salem Maya had many communities of support. She had her pastor the Reverend Serenus T. Churn and her fellow congregants at Mount Zion Baptist Church. There were her friends and colleagues at Wake Forest, as well as a host of locals with whom she'd formed close ties. And there was always her work.

The year she moved to North Carolina, *The Heart of a Woman,* the fourth book in her autobiographical series was published. In this volume Maya shared the energy and excitement of those early years in New York when she joined the Harlem Writers Guild, became an activist championing an end to segregation and African independence, and fell in love with Vus Make. But it is also about a woman claiming her own sovereignty, claiming her

A family gathering: Maya with her mother, Vivian, and stepfather, Knowledge Wilburn ("Papa Knowledge"), and son, Guy. *(Angelou-Johnson Family Archives)*

identity as an African American in the midst of an odyssey that would take her to Egypt and Ghana.

Another book of poetry, *Shaker, Why Don't You Sing,* and a delightful children's book, *Mrs. Flowers,* recalling that special friendship she shared, would follow in 1983. And Maya was soon at work on her fifth memoir detailing the years she lived in Ghana in the early 1960s—*All God's Children Need Traveling Shoes*—which was published in 1986. A year later there was another book of poetry in print, *Now Sheba Sings the Song,* which she described as "a play on the Song of Solomon. We never heard Sheba's song." And she asked a friend whom she'd first met when the two were expatriates in Ghana, the artist Tom Feelings, to provide the art.

In an interview with a writer for the *New York Times* in 1987, Maya offered a glimpse of her life. An early riser, her mornings were usually spent at home reading the newspaper and reviewing her correspondence with her secretary.

> I usually invite friends over [for lunch]. I'm a very serious cook and I prepare what to me is a fabulous meal. . . . I offer good wine and we laugh. . . . In the afternoon I read—if I'm teaching I read works coming out of the theme of my class and I put on music to compliment the reading.
>
> [At the close of the day,] I help myself to a very nice

drink . . . and I look at my paintings.
I'm a collector of Black American
art and I have paintings throughout
my house. . . . I prepare a proper
dinner and put on candles and pretty
music—all for me. . . . If I go out I
like to go to friends'.

When I'm writing, everything
shuts down. I get up about five, take
a shower . . . get in my car and drive
off to a hotel room. . . . I ask them to
take everything off the walls so there's me, the Bible,
Roget's Thesaurus, and some good, dry sherry and I'm at
work by 6:30. I write on the bed lying down—one elbow
is dark, really black from leaning on it—and I write in
longhand on yellow pads.

Maya and a dear friend,
artist and author Tom
Feelings. *(Angelou-Johnson
Family Archives)*

After a morning spent writing she would return home
and "pretend to be sane. . . . I play a lot of solitaire—in a
month when I'm writing I use two or three decks of cards.
After dinner I reread what I've written . . . eight o'clock is
the cruelest hour because that's when I start to edit"
(Carol Sarler, "A Day in the Life of Maya Angelou," *New
York Times Magazine,* December 27, 1987).

Her "traveling shoes" were also in constant use. Countless
speaking engagements filled her calendar. There were always trips
to California to be with family and friends, and visits to New York

A Pledge to Rescue our Youth

Young Women, young men of color, we
add our voices to those of your
ancestors who speak to you over ancient
seas and across impossible mountain tops

Come up from the gloom of national
neglect. You have already been seen.

Come out of the shadow of irrational
prejudice. You owe no racial debt to
its history.

The blood of our bodies and the
of our souls have bought for you a
future free from shame and beyond
beyond the telling of it.

We pledge ourselves and our resources
seek for you clean and well furnished
schools, safe and non threatening streets,
employment which makes use of
your talents but does not degrade
your dignity

You are the best we have
You are all we have
You are what we have become

We pledge you our whole hearts from
this day forward.

                    MA

Because We have inherited a culture
Which has resisted every attempt to destroy
Because we have inherited a self love
Survived our own annihilation
We accept our selves as Moral
support to the to and for the million
of young of am from girls
young to our young who
have a crying need for

---

our culture has sustained us
have inherited a culture
taining it has resisted destruction
have inherited a self love
which it has survived monumental
ampts to annihilate.

accept and for
ourselves as supporters
young women &
men who have a crying
for us

We know that courage is

A larger world may regard
our children as industrial waste
We see them as inheritors of the
spirit of David Walker - Harriet Tubman

(LEFT) Maya with her grandson, Colin. (*Angelou-Johnson Family Archives*)

(OPPOSITE) Maya wrote "A Pledge to Rescue Our Youth" for the Essence Music Festival in 2006 and it has been widely circulated by community and church groups ever since.

to meet with her editors, make public appearances, and spend easy time with friends.

Maya had grown increasingly fond of England and at least once a year she headed to London. She appreciated English eccentricities, the rich use of language, and the history. Her books were well received, as were the special programs she had done for the British Broadcasting Company, and Maya was held in high esteem as an artist and public intellectual. And as is true of every place she's ever spent time, she had a solid circle of friends.

And although she'd distanced herself from Hollywood, she continued to pursue her goal of directing, as well as writing, for the stage and film. Wearing one or both of those hats, she worked on productions in local and regional theaters, including a musical, *And Still I Rise*, that she wrote and eventually staged in Winston-Salem. And in London she directed *Moon on a Rainbow Shawl*. Considered a classic akin to Lorraine Hansberry's *A Raisin in the Sun*, Errol

(RIGHT) When the Bay Area writers planned to rally against apartheid, Maya and Jessica Mitford got right into the thick of things: "Decca called and said 'How about going to jail?' and I called Alice Walker and asked her to join us and Whoopi Goldberg came along." *(Photo by Pele deLappe)*

(OPPOSITE) The author signing books and greeting fans as she's done hundreds of times over the years. *(Angelou-Johnson Family Archives)*

John's play captures the life of a working-class neighborhood in Trinidad.

Sixty is the age when many people begin to think about retirement, but Maya was just picking up steam. There were yellow writing pads waiting to be filled, plays to direct, classes to teach, and thousands of men, women, and children across the country eagerly filling auditoriums and churches, banquet halls and theaters to hear her speak.

Then as now, many people come to hear her after reading her books, and they often bring copies in the hope that she will sign them. Others have seen her on television or read one of the many interviews she's given. All are eager to hear this multitalented woman, who in the course of her speeches often uses poetry and song, encourages laughter and reflection as she addresses history and art, challenges the group to rise above petty prejudices, repudi-

ates oppression, and celebrates being a woman, being Black, being courageous, being human. Maya often ends her speeches with one hand raised, finger pointing skyward exulting "And Still I Rise!" the refrain from one of her most beloved poems.

Indeed!

Maya was months away from her sixty-fifth birthday, when the newly elected William Jefferson Clinton asked her to write and deliver a poem at his inauguration, a great honor and a symbolic moment for these two people from Arkansas: the man from a place called Hope and the woman raised in Stamps are both from humble beginnings, both extraordinary, daring achievers. They were two Americans, their childhood's shaped in the South, now at the peak of their chosen careers, who had each worked and were working to make "a more perfect union," the promise of the Declaration of Independence, a living truth.

Not since Robert Frost at President Kennedy's inauguration had a poet been invited to take part in the ceremony. She'd struggled on the poem, holing up for weeks in her hotel room in Winston-Salem, filling more than five yellow pads, calling her friends for words of support when her confidence seemed to be flagging. This writer still vividly recalls the day Maya called asking

The Presidential Inaugural Committee
requests the honor of your presence
to attend and participate
in the
Inauguration of
William Jefferson Clinton
as
President of the United States of America
and
Albert Gore, Jr.
as
Vice President of the United States of America
on Wednesday, the twentieth of January
one thousand nine hundred and ninety-three
in the City of Washington

me to listen to the finished work. "She said, 'Sister, I hope that I didn't disturb you, I would appreciate it if you would listen to this and tell me what you think.' And then she read the poem. When she finished there was a long silence which prompted her to ask, 'Marcia are you still there?' I was in tears and it took me a moment to collect myself before I could respond. I was so proud of her, so moved by her message of hope and possibility, her vision. And I felt so honored that she was sharing it with me and asking my opinion."

Of that cold January morning when she stood before the nation and world she said, "I tried not to realize where I was. I tried to suspend myself. I was afraid I might lose my composure."

What followed was sheer magic. Here's how one writer, Kate Kelloway, described it in an article for a British publication: "She

Meeting in the Oval Office at the White House to discuss Black women's issues with the president. From left to right: C. DeLores Tucker, Dr. Dorothy Height, President Clinton, Alexis Herman, and Maya Angelou. *(Photo courtesy of the White House)*

DOING HER WORK

137

Moments after delivering the rousing poem "On the Pulse of Morning" that she wrote for the inauguration in 1993, Maya is thanked by the new president, William Jefferson Clinton. *(Photo courtesy of the White House)*

looked magnificent, sternly theatrical with an unsmiling bow mouth. She wore a coat with brass buttons, a strange reminder of the eight-year-old Maya Angelou who stood in a courtroom, terrified at the sight of the man who had raped her" (Kate Kelloway, "Poet for the New America," the *Observer,* January 24, 1993). As Kelloway noted, Maya had worn a similar coat on that fateful day, a navy blue coat with brass buttons, which she described in *Caged Bird* as "a friend that I hugged to me in the strange and unfriendly place."

But standing tall on the steps of the Capitol, she was light-years removed from that terrible time, and America was no longer an "unfriendly place." Her poem "On the Pulse of Morning" was a soaring call for peace, justice, and harmony. Capturing the hope embodied in the human spirit, it was a solemn and joyful reminder that all things are possible. She wished us "Good morning" in her poem, and one felt as if a new day was truly dawning.

Maya Angelou had long been greeting each new day with her arms wide, her spirit open, daring to live with hope and to test her courage as an artist, as an activist, as an intellectual, as a teacher, as a woman, as a human being. It was the heart and spirit of the woman, her dazzling intellect, wisdom and faith, her humor and laughter, as much as the power of her writing, that captured the hearts of millions of viewers whenever she appeared on Oprah Winfrey's television show. These two phenomenal women were a perfect pair, their mutual love and admiration blossoming into a true mother-daughter bonding.

Maya clearly remembers the first time they met. Oprah was the anchor of a local television news show in Baltimore.

She called and asked if she could interview me when I came to town to do a lecture at Morgan State University. I told her that I was pressed for time, but after she assured me that she would come there and only take five minutes, I agreed. At the exact time we'd set, there she was. She'd took me to an adjoining room where she'd set up a table and a comfortable chair with a pillow for me. And we immediately began. When she asked her first question and I answered, instead of racing on to another subject as interviewers too often do, she asked a question based on my prior response. She really listened, and we had a real conversation. And she finished her interview in exactly five

minutes. Just as she'd promised she would. I knew that she was going far.

Then shortly after she went to Chicago to do the show, I was in the city and saw her on the street, and walked up and said "Hello, Oprah Winfrey." She couldn't believe that I remembered her and knew her name—back then folks often mispronounced it. And then I called her and invited her to my home in North Carolina. She and Steadman came to spend a weekend, and that first night there were [the] three of us in our pajamas sitting on the floor in my living room reading poetry aloud.

—AS TOLD TO MARCIA ANN GILLESPIE

It was love!

Like Maya, Oprah had spent her early years in the care of a grandmother in the South, fallen in love with books, memorized favorite poems, been sexually victimized as a child, and had floundered for a time before finding her footing. These two magnificent survivors are both optimists with feisty spirits, an abundance of courage, profound spiritual faith, and boundless belief in the human spirit. Generous and joyful, they also share a love of laughter, silly games, good jokes, great parties, and a commitment to making a positive difference in the lives of others.

Maya's appearance on Oprah's show brought her great attention and a wider audience. She was famous before and even more so after. But nothing had prepared her for the avalanche of public acclaim that followed on the heels of that inaugural day.

While Maya enjoyed the attention, she remained a committed

(OPPOSITE) Maya and her chosen daughter Oprah held a pajama party on one of Winfrey's shows in 1997. (Photo by George Burns © 1997 Harpo Productions, Inc.)

swimmer, constantly testing new waters. There were new books: a collection of poetry, *I Shall Not Be Moved* (1990); poems for children, *Life Doesn't Frighten Me*, illustrated by Jean-Michel Basquiat (1993); and a series of essays on living, *Wouldn't Take Nothing for My Journey Now* (1993). She'd also written the poetry featured in John Singleton's 1992 film *Poetic Justice* and, to the delight of her fans, accepted a key role in the film. Within months of the inauguration, a bound volume of her poem "On the Pulse of Morning" would be rushed into print in response to public demand.

Keeping faithful to the advice her mother had given her years before to "Just do your work" Maya kept stepping up. She recorded her inaugural poem and won a Grammy Award for it. In 1995 she followed with the much acclaimed *Phenomenal Woman: Four Poems*

Winona Ryder (center) and Ellen Burstyn (right) were two of Maya's costars along with Anne Bancroft and Alfre Woodard in the 1995 TV film *How to Make an American Quilt. (Photo © 1995 Universal City Studios, Inc., and Amblin Entertainment, Inc. Courtesy of Universal Studios Licensing LLLP)*

Celebrating Women and garnered another Grammy for the recorded version. And again the world took notice when the United Nations asked Maya Angelou to deliver a poem to commemorate its fiftieth anniversary in 1995. That poem, "A Brave and Startling Truth" was published the same year. Two more children's books followed in 1996: *My Painted House, My Friendly Chicken, and Me* and *Kofi and His Magic* (in collaboration with Margaret Courtney Clarke).

She took on other acting assignments. A guest role on the then popular TV drama, *Touched by an Angel* (1995), gave her the opportunity to work with her old friend Della Reese, whose singing years before had been the catalyst in Maya's decision to focus on her writing. She was one of the wise women starring in the film *How to Make an American Quilt:* her cast mates included Ellen Burstyn, Alfre Woodard, and Winona Ryder. And the Film Board and BBC of Scotland turned to Maya to commemorate the bicentennial anniversary of the poet Robert Burns, whose poetry she has cherished since childhood, in the documentary *Angelou on Burns.* The documentary traces Maya's poetic journey from her home in Stamps,

(LEFT) A scene from the 1996 documentary *Angelou on Burns*, a bicentennial tribute to Scottish poet Robert Burns that aired on the BBC network in 1996. *(Photo: Taylored Productions Ltd.)*

Maya had long wanted to direct a feature-length film and that dream was realized with *Down in the Delta* (1998). *(Courtesy Miramax Films)*

Arkansas, to Burns's home in Ayrshire, Scotland, and features her sipping scotch and sharing songs with the locals, and reciting many of her favorite Burns poems in an impeccable brogue.

In 1996, the same year the Burns documentary aired, Maya was also wowing music fans on the album *Been Found*, which she'd done in collaboration with her dear friends, the singer-songwriters Nick Ashford and Valerie

Simpson. To the delight of audiences, she joined them on stage at several of their concerts. And finally Maya Angelou achieved the one goal that had long eluded her, when she was asked to direct *Down in the Delta*, a feature film scheduled for wide release. Maya recruited a sterling group of actors—Mary Alice, Al Freeman Jr., Esther Rolle (in what would be her final appearance), Alfre Woodard, and Wesley Snipes—for this moving family drama.

Many years earlier, when asked the source of her creative diversity, Maya Angelou replied, "I think talent is like electricity."

Some of us never tap into the current, perhaps fearful of the voltage. Maya Angelou stepped into the new century, calling on the lightning, embracing the energy, bursting to share her gifts and test her creativity, eagerly taking on new projects—still swimming, still doing her work.

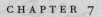

CHAPTER 7

Life as Art

Living well is an art which can be developed.

—MAYA ANGELOU (1993)

for a few month I was a novelty
then attendance began to wane
I was told that people had gone
...close to listen to a real singer
...riosity led me. Then came a night
...en there was a decided drop in
...eness. Night after night attenda
...egan to wane until it became
...mon to find the club over at
...ll at showtime I was told the
rival had hired an ...
...thentic singer. I went alone to
... to see my competition and the
... show made me come to
...eps with my life.

    Della Reese was announced an
...en she appeared there was an
...dible gasp. She was nearly six feet
...ll and very beautiful and was
...aring what could be called a gr...
...own. There were no sequins or ...
...shiny stars on her dress. She was
...tainly not dressed ...

A LITTLE GIRL NAMED MARGUERITE JOHNSON growing up in Stamps, Arkansas, in the 1930s dreamed of living in the world. She treasured the few books that she had, memorizing them, savoring the words, imagining what her life might be like if she were one of the characters, imagining herself in a different place, a different time. Books were her refuge and her salvation but she never imagined that her words would one day stir a nation, be treasured by people in far flung places around the world.

When Marguerite Johnson Angelos changed her name to Maya Angelou it was to earn a living. She never imagined that hers was to become a household name, that her life's journey would inspire millions, that as Maya Angelou she would be hailed as "the people's poet." Scrambling to pay the rent she never envisioned the wealth and acclaim that would be hers or that "her work and, given the nature of her work, also her life," as one writer described it, would "have effectively been branded. The pain of her early years, and the wisdom she has derived from it, has been commodified" (Gary Younge, "No Surrender," *The Guardian,* May 25, 2002).

Maya Angelou is an artist, dedicated, driven, always pushing herself, and she is also a shrewd businesswoman who makes no apologies for her material success. "I agree with Balzac and nineteenth-century writers, Black and White, who say, 'I write for money,' " she laughs. "Yes, I think everybody should be paid handsomely, I insist on it and I pay people who work for me, or with me, handsomely" (Younge, "No Surrender").

She lives in a large sprawling house in Winston-Salem, each

art-filled room a burst of color, one floor reserved for guests, her growing library on another. There's a separate guest house on the property, and a greenhouse reserved for the orchids she loves, a sculpture garden, a gazebo. The first home she bought in Winston-Salem is not far away; it serves as guest house and office. Her executive assistant, staff of secretaries, and her papers occupy one floor. Her niece, Rosa Johnson Butler, who is

her aunt's archivist, maintains an office there. Maya owns two brownstones in Harlem in New York City. She converted one into apartments. The other she bought for her own use. Little more than a shell when she purchased it, she painstakingly transformed it into a showplace: a private elevator, a huge and welcoming state-of-the-art kitchen, a dining room with clouds painted on the ceiling.

When in New York or on the road Dr. Angelou, as she prefers to be called by people other than friends or family, is attended by her personal assistant, Lydia Stuckey. She employs a full-time cook-housekeeper, a cleaning staff, a gardener, a chauffeur. She keeps a mini fleet of classic Lincoln sedans. She has her own bus—manned

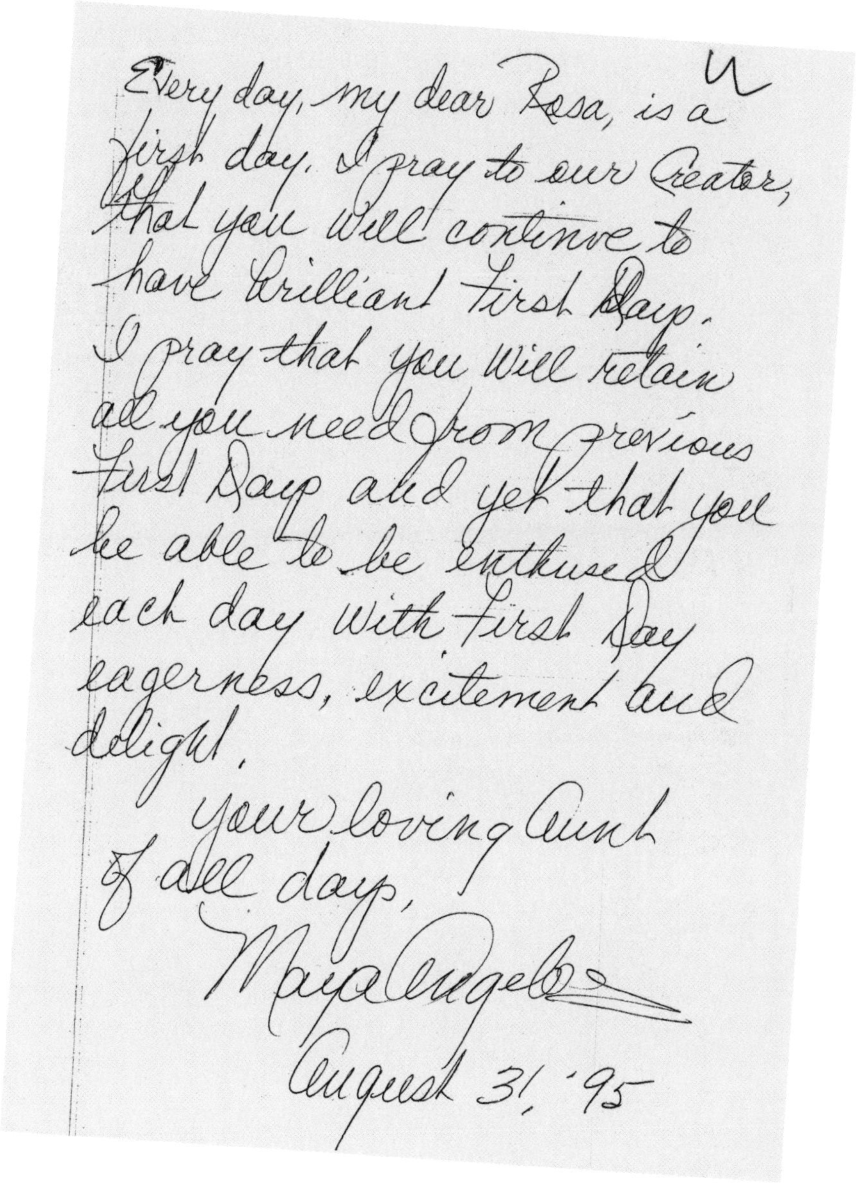

Every day, my dear Rosa, is a
first day. I pray to our Creator,
that you will continue to
have brilliant first days.
I pray that you will retain
all you need from previous
first days and yet that you
be able to be enthused
each day with first day
eagerness, excitement and
delight.
        your loving Aunt
of all day,
        Maya Angelou

August 31, '95

A note to her niece, Rosa
Johnson Butler, when she
went back to college to get
her degree.

by two drivers—the newest of them has been custom-designed. Kente cloth adorns the walls, the sides expand, there's a commodious kitchen, a private bedroom, comfortable couches, bunk beds for the drivers— a home on the road. She lives well, enjoys the fruits of her labor, and takes great delight in sharing it all with her family and friends.

But the material goods neither define nor inspire her. "Strength, love, courage, love, kindness, love. That is really what matters."

Throughout her life, as in her work, Maya Angelou has affirmed and celebrated the threads that bind us one to another. She believes in us, the human family, with our rainbow of emotions, our complex imaginations. She believes in the boundless capacity of our spirits and the hope and possibility in each and every breath that we take. She wants the best from us and from herself, the best for us and for herself, knowing that we struggle, sometimes falter, stumble, lose our way.

In her autobiographical writing she has shared many of her struggles and stumbles, along with her triumphs, ever mindful and reminding us of the role others play in our lives. People—family,

LIFE AS ART

friends, acquaintances, co-workers, young and old—who directly or indirectly provide valuable life lessons, offer support when it is most needed. People who challenge, inspire, move her: At every stage and phase of her life Maya tells us about the people she's met, the lessons learned, the laughter, and sometimes tears, shared. "The sisters and brothers that you meet give you the materials which your character uses to build itself. It is said that some people are born great, others achieve it, some have it thrust upon them. In truth, the ways in which your character is built have to do with all three of those. Those around you, those you choose, and those who choose you" (as told to Marcia Ann Gillespie).

Her family remains first in her heart. Mention her mother's name and her eyes light up, her laughter bubbles. Lady B, who died in 1991, spent her last years with Maya in North Carolina, feisty, charming, and witty right to the end. Maya loves telling BB stories to friends, who in turn often urge her to write a book sharing her mother's signature wit, wisdom, and chutzpah with her readers. She also brought her brother, Bailey, to Winston-Salem in 1998, after he suffered a series of debilitating strokes. Respectful of his need for independence, she settled him in her first house and hired round-the-clock care. Bailey spent the last twenty-two months of his life with his sister, My.

(OPPOSITE) Getting ready to step out in Winston-Salem with her "big" brother, Bailey Johnson, who moved to North Carolina and spent his declining years with his beloved sister. (Photo © M. Courtney-Clarke)

(BELOW) Maya amidst the ever-growing Angelou-Johnson family: (from left to right) Maya's grandson, Colin, holding son Brandon Bailey and his wife, Jessica, with Caylin; Guy and his wife, Stephanie; and Maya's brother Bailey's firstborn, her niece, Rosa Johnson Butler. (Angelou-Johnson Family Archives)

Four generations: A beaming Maya with son, Guy (center); grandson, Colin; and great-granddaughter, Caylin, at a family gathering in 2000. *(Photo by Susan J. Ross)*

Her own mother pride and love is boundless when it comes to her son. As a result of those accidents years ago, Guy Johnson has had to endure a series of spinal surgeries and lives with almost constant pain. One would never know it, as he, like his mother, never complains. He stands tall, with a quiet strength and a deep peaceful center, a fierce independent streak and a great sense of humor, like his mother. He is also a thoughtful speaker, a careful listener, an avid reader, and an accomplished published writer, again like his mother, the woman he described as "the Lady with seven-league boots," when he dedicated his first novel to her: "You who have taught me there is no end of learning, to growing, to reaching higher, to pursuing the right path, and perhaps greater, that all pursuits are lost if there is no love, no investment in others" (Guy Johnson, *Standing at the Scratch Line*, Random House, 1998).

Guy and his wife, Stephanie, live in the Oakland–Bay Area but travel east frequently to be with Maya. Mother and son have a close but not clingy relationship. Each is respectful of the other's breathing space, deeply proud of the other; they are always championing and cheering each other on.

And though she missed a crucial part of his childhood, Maya was there to share the vicissitudes of her grandson Colin's adolescence, to offer her toast at his marriage, celebrate his graduation from college, and shed tears of joy at the births of his children. Like her Grandmother Henderson, she offers Colin, who's a budding entrepreneur, counsel and encouragement, words to live by, standards to aspire to, nononsense advice. One can almost see her swell when she speaks about the joy she takes in her great-grand-children, Caylin Nicole and Brandon Bailey Johnson. She dotes on her "little ones" showers them with presents and, far more precious, her wisdom and life lessons and love.

An intimate teaching moment: Maya passing pearls of wisdom to her great-granddaughter, Caylin. *(Photo by Susan J. Ross)*

Key to those lessons will be the importance of loving others, as she has done throughout her journey. Maya has kept her arms wide open, reaching out to embrace chosen family and friends. Writers,

actors, singers and dancers, musicians and poets, intellectuals, activists and journalists, artists and producers, directors, politicians, teachers and chefs, photographers, choreographers, entrepreneurs and business professionals, just folks and the world famous gather round her table, savoring food, sharing laughter, and swapping stories. When asked about her friendships she often says, "Many years ago my mother told me, 'If you want to have a friend, you have to be a friend.' I've followed her advice, and I strive to be a good friend" (as told to Marcia Ann Gillespie).

(ABOVE) Decorating Easter eggs with (from left to right) niece, Rosa, friends Lynn Cothran and Phoebe Beasley, and Rosa's husband, Danny Butler. *(Angelou-Johnson Family Archives)*

(RIGHT) Sharing a laugh with Rosa Parks, the Civil Rights legend. Maya considered Parks to be a national treasure. *(Angelou-Johnson Family Archives)*

Some people form fast friendships that quickly spark and then just as quickly fade. Maya Angelou's friendships tend to endure because she remains ever mindful of their importance and expects the same care and concern in return. In her writing she has chosen to share much of her life with her readers, but she is at the same time a very private person and a great respecter of the privacy of others. She would never dream of revealing anything said to her in confidence. And no matter how busy she may be, there is always time to listen if a friend calls in need of her attention. Ask her opinion or her advice and only after careful consideration will she give it. But she never seems to judge. She is not a gossip and actively discourages others from gossiping around her.

A gathering of friends and family at Alex Haley's farm in Tennessee. *(Photo © by poet Eugene Redmond. Used by permission of Eugene B. Redmond)*

She believes in giving respect to one's elders, in using formal address calling and introducing adults as "Mr." or "Mrs.," "Miss" or "Ms." Good manners matter to Maya and she's quick to correct you—nicely, but firmly—if you cross the line. She describes herself as being "extremely formal. I hope not starchily so, but I do not encourage familiarity. I encourage closeness, but not familiarity" (as told to Marcia Ann Gillespie).

(ABOVE) Maya with sister writers Rosa Guy and Louise Meriwether on one of their sojourns together in North Carolina. *(Photo © by poet Eugene Redmond. Used by permission of Eugene B. Redmond)*

(RIGHT) For several years Maya maintained a home in Atlanta, Georgia. At one of the many parties she hosted while living there she paused for this photo with Amina Baraka at her side, Val Gray Ward, and the writers Sonia Sanchez and Mari Evans. *(Photo © by poet Eugene Redmond. Used by permission of Eugene B. Redmond)*

There are some things that she will not tolerate, like bad manners, mean-spiritedness, cruelty, racism. "I will not sit in a group of Black friends and hear racial pejoratives against Whites. I will not hear 'honky.' I will not hear 'Jap.' I will not hear 'kike.' I will not hear 'greaser.' I will not hear 'dago.' I will not hear it. I will not have gay bashing, lesbian bashing. Not

in my company. As soon as I hear it, I say, 'Excuse me, I have to leave. Sorry.' Or if it's in my home, I say, 'You have to leave. I can't have that. That is poison, and I know it is poison, and you're smearing it on me. I will not have it' " (Academy of Achievement interview, January 22, 1997).

It should come as no surprise that many of Maya's extended family are artists and writers. But had she never put pen to paper, stepped foot on a stage, kicked up her heels in dance Maya Angelou would still have made friendship a priority, would still have created a large chosen family. People matter to her. She is unstinting with her praise for those whom she admires and greatly values people of good heart and open spirit. People who are thoughtful. People who share her zest for life.

Here Maya poses in 1996 with her dear friends the legendary singer-composers Nick Ashford and Valerie Simpson for their album *Been Found*. *(Photo © Aaron Rapoport Photography.)*

Wherever she happens to be nesting, Maya delights in gathering her friends around her to celebrate special occasions or simply celebrate being together. She's a generous and thoughtful host—remembering friends' favorite foods and special diets—and an extraordinary cook, whose repertoire ranges from West Africa to Europe to the American South. (The one thing missing from her table is seafood, because she's extremely allergic to anything from the sea.) Although she no longer does all the heavy lifting in the kitchen these days, the recipes are always hers and she keeps an eye on all the pots.

Every Thanksgiving she and her Johnson family (son Guy, grandson Colin, and niece Rosa and their spouses) host a weekend gathering in Winston-Salem and, in addition to their family, invite the extended Angelou clan of friends and chosen family. It's an international, multiracial, intergenerational tribe several hundred members strong.

(ABOVE) One of the events Maya, shown here cavorting poolside, always looked forward to was Nick Ashford and Valerie Simpson's annual Fourth of July "all white" party. *(Angelou-Johnson Family Archives)*

(RIGHT) When Toni Morrison (center) received the Nobel Prize for her novel *Beloved*, Maya held a party in her honor. Here the hostess and honoree pose with the poet Rita Dove. *(Photo © by poet Eugene Redmond. Used by permission of Eugene B. Redmond)*

Ratatouille

2 tablespoons olive oil

1 large yellow onion, diced

3 garlic cloves, minced

2 eggplants, cut into 8 pieces each

3 large green bell peppers, cut into large strips

3 large red bell peppers, cut into large strips

2 zucchini, each cut into 4 pieces

2 large tomatoes, peeled and diced

2 cups vegetable or chicken broth

2 yellow summer squash, each cut into 4 pieces

½ teaspoon dried marjoram

½ teaspoon dried oregano

1 teaspoon dried basil

½ teaspoon dried rosemary

1 teaspoon salt

Maya's recipe for one of her favorite vegetable dishes.

Heat the oil in a large saucepan over medium heat. Add the onions, garlic, and eggplant and sauté for 12 to 15 minutes. Add the remaining ingredients. Cover and simmer for 1 hour over low heat. Remove the cover and cook until liquid is reduced by two-thirds.

Five members of her New York family whom Maya particularly dotes on—George Faison, the celebrated director and choreographer and his life partner, T. Schnugg; Nick Ashford and Valerie Simpson, the mega-talented singer-songwriters; and their righthand woman, Tee Alston—are always in the thick of things helping to orchestrate the talent show and other special surprises. The weekend invariably includes music, dancing, song, goofy games, and great performances, and always concludes with prayer, thanks giving, and praise songs.

(ABOVE) Singer-song-writers Nick Ashford and Valerie Simpson collaborating with Maya on one of the songs for their album *Been Found*. *(Photo © by poet Eugene Redmond. Used by permission of Eugene B. Redmond)*

Maya is a woman of faith, her spiritual belief deeply held, first nurtured long ago in Stamps. "I believe that Spirit is one and is everywhere, present. That it is everywhere present. . . . I cannot separate what I conceive as Spirit from my concept of God. Thus I believe that God is Spirit" (Maya Angelou, *Lessons in Living*, interview by Marcia Ann Gillespie, *Essence*, December 1992).

And it is that sense of Spirit that Maya shares with but never presses on her friends. But she treats her closest friendships like a sacred trust and tends to them constantly.

Sisterhood and brotherhood is a condition people have to work at. It's a serious matter. You compromise, you give, you take, you stand firm, and you're relentless. The only thing is that you just don't have sex to complicate it. But all the responsibility, all the courtesy, all the soft and sweet words, all the teaching words, are called for in those relationships as much as in a love affair. It's a serious matter. It's big stuff. . . . It is an investment.

—STOKES OLIVER, "MAYA ANGELOU: THE HEART OF THE WOMAN"

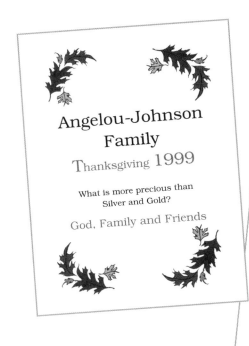

Invitations to Angelou-Johnson's annual Thanksgiving Celebrations: What began as a small gathering of family and friends over the years has grown into a glorious weekend-long affair.

Her readers have come to know some of her chosen family from her autobiographies. And one would be hard-pressed to find someone who isn't aware of the special mother-daughter bond she and Oprah Winfrey share. Theirs is a mutual love fest and their conversations on Oprah's show have had a profound impact on millions of viewers. Many women often refer to one show when Maya eased many of their fears about growing older when she laughingly referred to watching her once firm breasts race downward.

But when she talks about the importance of one's friendships, Maya is quick to remind "that only equals make friends" and to advise of the need to have among them "friends that one can count on to stand shoulder to shoulder with you if you were called to enter the lion's den." Among her many sister-friends, she knew three in particular would have been right there beside her—M. J. (Mary Jane) Hewitt, Dolly McPherson, and the late Jessica "Decca" Mitford. No wonder that when the editors of a woman's magazine asked to photograph and interview Maya and her "best friend" for a special feature, she responded that she had not one but three.

At the time, Dolly was teaching at Wake Forest University; M. J., an arts consultant, lived in Los Ange-

LIFE AS ART

Oprah Winfrey hosted a series of spectacular parties ranging from tented extravaganzas to a seven-day cruise to celebrate Maya's sixty-fifth, seventieth, and seventy-fifth birthdays.

(OPPOSITE) Here Maya enjoys the festivities with Oprah and Quincy Jones.

(THIS PAGE) With grandson, Colin; Dorothy Height and Robert A. Hall *(photos by Richard Shay)*; Tee Alston and Valerie Simpson *(photo by George Burns)*

les; and Decca, a writer famed for her exposés, in Berkeley. Maya's sister bonding with each of the three spans decades. Her friendship with M. J. Hewitt, dates back to the mid 1950s. They met when M. J. and a group of friends came to hear Maya sing at a nightclub in Beverly Hills. Maya was immediately struck by M. J.'s beauty and spirit: "She has the most extraordinary green eyes that sparked and snapped with so much intelligence, and such joie de vivre" (as told to Marcia Ann Gillespie). Like Maya, M. J. is a woman who chose to live in the world, an inveterate traveler and serious scholar. The two share a love of and extensive knowledge about black art and folklore, and a great zest for life. M. J., a fine arts curator and consultant and one of the nation's preeminent experts on African American art, is a former university professor and administrator. Over the years these sister-friends have collaborated on a number of projects to benefit visual artists.

Ask her to talk about her sister Maya and M. J. immediately begins to laugh as she shares one of her favorite Maya stories.

I was staying with sister Maya in North Carolina, and you know when she goes to bed at night that house gets locked up tight. She had another houseguest there who got up early one morning to go jogging but no

(OPPOSITE) When the editors of *Self* magazine asked her to pose with her best friend for an article in 1994, Maya told them that she had three. Here she is with her "sisters" (from left to right) Dolly McPherson, M. J. Hewitt, and Jessica Mitford. *(Photo © Jon Ragel/CORBIS OUTLINE)*

(BELOW) Maya and her "sister" M. J. Hewitt have been best friends for more than fifty years. They met when M. J. came to hear Maya sing at a club in Beverly Hills. *(Photo by Susan J. Ross)*

one knew that this was his routine. Well when he opened the front door all the alarms went off. I ran out in the hall and there was Maya standing at the top of the stairs in her nightgown with her pistol in hand ready to defend us all. And there was that man shaking in his jogging clothes! It was hilarious. And so like my brave sister.

—AS TOLD TO MARCIA ANN GILLESPIE

With her late sister-writer Jessica (Decca) Mitford Maya shared a love of great writing, a zest for games, most especially Boggle, and a passion for social justice. Decca, as she was affectionately called by those closest to her, became known as one of the nation's great muckrakers with her searing expose of the funeral industry, *The American Way of Death*. Maya was also very close to Decca's husband, Robert "Bob" Treuhaft, a tough-minded labor lawyer, who shared his wife's political and social passions. It would be Jessica,

4/4/96

Dearest Dec,

This day, my birthday, the day
after Ron Brown's death (he was
a friend) this day when I grieve
anew for Martin (who was killed
on this day 28 yrs ago) this
day, which I always begin with
a call from or to Coretta King (if
we don't speak on the third (3rd)
is a day for recalling beloved friends
and unexpected mercies. Of course
you and our years of devotion, tears
and laughter flood my thoughts.
I needed to tell you that I love
you and love having you in
my life, enriching my life
and influencing my life.
My always love to Bob
and congratulations to Ben
and affection to the Dinky-Dont
and hers.

Love, Maya

Maya says, who after going into the lion's den with her and "vanquishing the wild beast would run me crazy with 'Why the hell were you in that damn room in the first place?' "

Decca, whose ribald sense of humor often left Maya "laughing so hard that I cried," shared her sister-friend's sense of adventure, often daring and egging Maya on. When the Ringling Bros. and Barnum & Bailey circus came to the San Francisco Bay area in 1976 Maya was invited to ride an elephant in the opening-night parade. Folks who knew the two of them weren't in the least surprised that there was Decca riding another one beside her. And when Jessica,

then well into her seventies, embarked on a singing career in the mid-1990s forming her own group called Decca and the Deccatones, there was Maya cheering her on. As a lark, the two recorded a CD, *There Is a Moral to It All*, for Don't Quit Your Day Job Productions in 1996. It features the two of them singing two classic working-class British pub songs and an interview with Maya saying of her friend's singing, "She doesn't have a lot of musical acumen. But on the other hand, she has the courage, the concentration, of somebody about to be executed in the next half-hour."

The passing of Decca and Bob, like the death of anyone she holds dear, leaves Maya asking "What legacy was left which can help me in the art of living a good life?" Key to that good life is in embracing the families of her friends, as she'd done when she reached out to Martin Luther King's and Malcolm X's widows offering her friendship and support. Both Coretta Scott King and Betty Shabazz were among her closest sister-friends and Maya is an aunt to their children. Maya's a beloved sister to the Baldwin clan, aunt to Decca and Bob's daughter and family, and so many others. As

another of Maya's sisters, the distinguished educator Dr. Ruth Love says: "Maya takes the high road and moves ahead in life. And that is very instructive to people around her—never withholding anything always being forthright" (Margaret Courtney-Clarke, *Maya Angelou: The Poetry of Living*, Clarkson Potter, 2000).

Yet it would take the passage of more than three decades before Maya was able to write *A Song Flung Up to Heaven*, the sixth and final book in her autobiographical series for Random House. Writing this book in which she had to revisit the loss of Malcolm X and Martin Luther King Jr. proved so painful that Maya delayed the task, completing it only in 2002. "I agonized while writing that book. It was such a painful period. Malcolm and Martin were such courageous men. They were men who were willing to admit when they were wrong, who kept evolving. So much possibility lost."

When she completed that book Maya declared that she would not do another autobiography. But fortunately, for her many devoted readers and fans she hasn't stopped sharing her wisdom or her memories. She turned her attention to a project many friends and family had long urged her to tackle: She wrote a cookbook. In *Hallelujah, The Welcome Table: A Lifetime of Memories with Recipes* Maya talks as much about people as she does about food, reminding us as always that "we are more alike than unalike."

And she welcomed the new millennium by taking on a completely new venture. In an unprecedented arrangement with Hallmark she created a signature collection of cards for all occasions, date books and journals, gifts and collectibles called

> Maya Angelou's Life Mosaic. For many years, Hallmark asked me to do it, but I said no. Then I met the Hallmark people, and I liked them. I spoke to a person who figures heavily in my life and said, "I'm thinking of doing some work for Hallmark." He said, "You can't do that—you're the people's poet." After I got off the phone, I said, "Wait a minute—if I'm the people's poet, shouldn't I write for the people? There are people who never read a book, but I can get an idea over to them on a greeting card."
> —YOUNGE, "NO SURRENDER"

As she'd done time and time again, Maya Angelou refused to be boxed in, even by those who wished her well. She's the inaugural poet who rocks out on stage singing with Ashford and Simpson. She's the dancer turned Calypso Queen. Singer, actor, activist, reporter, poet, author, screenwriter, director, songwriter, teacher, producer, lecturer, entrepreneur—she's a woman with many hats, and wears them all with style, always looking for a new one to try on.

Though her dancer's legs don't always cooperate, Maya, wielding an elegant silver-headed walking stick and making light of her arthritic knees, keeps stepping. When one reporter asked how she was adjusting to this stage of her life, she responded by singing the final verse of her poem, "On Aging":

> *I'm the same person I was back then*
> *A little less hair, a little less chin,*
> *A lot less lungs and much less wind.*
> *But ain't I lucky I can still breathe in.*

Some people pack their dreams away like treasures in a hope chest, Maya keeps hers close, tries them out, dreams anew. In countless interviews over the years, Maya has spoken about how much she values courage and respects those who act courageously, saying that "courage is the most important of all the virtues, because without courage you can't practice any other virtue consistently" (as told to Marcia Ann Gillespie).

In her writing, speeches, and conversations she is always encouraging us to be fully present, to "be as honest and courageous and as courteous and as loving as you can be." She calls us to have the courage to love, to dare to try something new, to step up and stand up for ourselves, to seek to explore and achieve our potential. It's how she lives her life.

As she celebrates her eightieth birthday, Maya Angelou greets each new day hopeful, open to new adventures, ready to learn, love, laugh, and share, eager to do her work.

In an interview more than three decades ago Maya talked about the importance of work in her life, and what she said is as true today as it was then: "I appreciate the popularity of my work, but I don't believe it. I *dare* not! I say 'Thank you, that's very nice of you, but where's my next work? What am I supposed to be doing now?' " (Sheila Weller, "Work in Progress: Maya Angelou," *Intellectual Digest,* June 1973).

We who love her reply, Keep Rising Maya, Keep Rising!

for a few month I was a novelty
then the attendance began to wane
I was told that people had gone
other club to listen to a real singer
curiosity led me. Then came a Negro
when there was a decided drop in
business. Night after night attenda
began to wane until it became
common to find the club over at
ll at showtime. I was told that
rival _____ had hired an _____
thentic singer. I went alone to
_____ the competition and the
_____ show made me come to
terms with my life.
Della Reese was announced an
when she _____ appeared there was an
incredible gasp. She was nearly six feet
ll and very beautiful and was
aring what could be called a pro
own. There were no sequins or bea
or phony stars on her dress. She was

ACKNOWLEDGMENTS

From Marcia Ann Gillespie

This book would not have been possible were it not for the generosity of my big sister, friend, and mentor, Maya Angelou, who opened her arms wide to embrace this project and this writer.

Many thanks to Robert Levine who made it possible for me to write this book.

All praises to our editor, Janet Hill, for her unwavering commitment, enthusiasm, and belief in this book.

Special bouquets to all of my friends and family who urged me on when my spirits flagged.

From Rosa Johnson Butler

To my loving children, Alvin, Shelby (deceased), Olivia, and Helena: Thank you for choosing me to be your mother.

To Janet Hill, much love and respect for your continued encouragement and your consistent belief in this important book.

Love to Aunt Dolly for your laughter.

Love to Jane Stephens and Susan von Cannon, for our sessions together.

Much love to all my beloveds and extended family members.

A special hug to my only cousin, Guy Johnson, and his beautiful wife, Stephanie Floyd Johnson.

All is well.

FROM RICHARD A. LONG

Thanks so much to Eleanor Traylor, Dolly McPherson, Guy and Stephanie Johnson, Nick Ashford and Valerie Simpson, and Carolyn Clark.

ABOUT THE AUTHORS

Writer and journalist MARCIA ANN GILLESPIE, is a longtime friend of Dr. Angelou's. Gillespie was the editor in chief of *Essence* magazine from 1971 to 1980 and the driving force behind the magazine's early success. The former editor in chief of *Ms.* magazine (1993–2002), she lives in New York City. Gillespie is currently working on her memoir.

ROSA JOHNSON BUTLER is Dr. Angelou's niece and archivist. Her father, the late Bailey Johnson, is the brother and mentor Angelou writes about in *I Know Why the Caged Bird Sings* and her other autobiographical works. Johnson Butler is currently engaged in graduate work in archival studies and program design, and speaks often to educational civic groups. She is married to Daniel Butler and lives in Winston-Salem, North Carolina.

RICHARD A. LONG has known Maya Angelou for more than thirty years. A cultural historian, he is the author of *African Americans: A Portrait* (preface by Maya Angelou), *The Black Tradition in American Dance,* and *Grown Deep: Essays on the Harlem Renaissance* (dedicated to Maya Angelou). He is the Atticus Haygood Professor of Interdisciplinary Studies, Emeritus, at Emory University. He lives in Atlanta.

for a few month I was a novelty
then ... attendance began to wane
... was told that people had ...
other club to listen to a real singer
... curiosity led me. Then came a night
... there was a decided drop ...
...eness. Night after night attendance
began to wane until it became
common to find the club only ...
... at showtime I was told that ...
rival ... had hired an ...
...thentic singer. I went alone to ...
... see my competition and the
... show made me come to
grips with my life.
Della Reese was announced and
when she ... appeared there was an
incredible gasp. She was nearly six feet
tall and very beautiful and was
wearing what could be called a ...
gown. There were no sequins or ...
or shiny stars on her dress. She was

THE WORKS OF MAYA ANGELOU

AUTOBIOGRAPHY

I Know Why the Caged Bird Sings
Random House, 1970

Gather Together in My Name
Random House, 1974

Singin' and Swingin' and Gettin'
Merry Like Christmas
Random House, 1976

The Heart of a Woman
Random House, 1981

All God's Children Need
Traveling Shoes
Random House, 1986

A Song Flung Up to Heaven
Random House, 2002

I Know Why the Caged Bird Sings:
The Collected Autobiographies
of Maya Angelou
Modern Library, 2004

PERSONAL ESSAY

Wouldn't Take Nothing for
My Journey Now
Random House, 1993

Even the Stars Look Lonesome
Random House, 1997

Hallelujah! The Welcome Table: A
Lifetime of Memories with Recipes
Random House, 2004

Mother: A Cradle to Hold Me
Random House, 2006

CHILDREN'S BOOKS

Life Doesn't Frighten Me
Stewart, Tabori and Chang, 1993

My Painted House, My Friendly
Chicken and Me
Clarkson Potter, 1994

Kofi and His Magic
Clarkson Potter, 1996

MAYA'S WORLD:
Izak of Lapland
Random House, 2004

MAYA'S WORLD:
Angelina of Italy
Random House, 2004

MAYA'S WORLD:
Renée Marie of France
Random House, 2004

MAYA'S WORLD:
Mikale of Hawaii
Random House, 2004

POETRY

Just Give Me a Cool Drink of
Water 'Fore I Diiie
Random House, 1971

Oh Pray My Wings Are Gonna
Fit Me Well
Random House, 1975

And Still I Rise
Random House, 1978

Shaker, Why Don't You Sing?
Random House, 1983

Poems
Bantam, 1986

Now Sheba Sings the Song
Random House, 1987

I Shall Not Be Moved
Random House, 1990

"On the Pulse of Morning"
This poem was written at the request of
William Jefferson Clinton and recited at
his inauguration as the forty-second
president of the United States, January
20, 1993, and was published by Random
House in March 1993.

The Complete Collected Poems
of Maya Angelou
Random House, 1994

Phenomenal Woman:
Four Poems for Women
Random House, 1995

A Brave and Startling Truth
Random House, 1995
Recited at the celebration of the fiftieth
anniversary of the United Nations on
June 26, 1995

"From a Black Woman
to a Black Man"
Delivered at the Million Man March in
Washington, D.C., on October 16, 1995

Amazing Peace
Random House, 2005
Read at the ceremony lighting the
national Christmas tree at the White
House on December 1, 2005

Mother: A Cradle to Hold Me
Random House, 2006

Celebrations: Rituals for Peace
and Prayer
Random House, 2006

Poetry for Young People:
Maya Angelou
Sterling Publishing, 2007

PLAYS

Cabaret for Freedom
1960 (in collaboration with
Godfrey Cambridge)

The Least of These
1966

Getting' Up Stayed on My Mind
1967

Sophocles' Ajax
1974 (adaptation)

And I Still Rise
1976 (writer/director)

Moon on a Rainbow Shawl
1988 (adapted from the book
by Errol John)

Georgia, Georgia
Independent-Cinerama, 1972

All Day Long
American Film Institute, 1974
(writer/director)

I Know Why the Caged Bird Sings
CBS-TV, 1979 (writer for script
and musical score)

Sister, Sister
NBC-TV, 1982

Brewster Place
Harpo Productions, 1990
(writer for series)

PBS Documentaries: *Who Cares About
Kids & Kindred Spirits,*
KERA-TV, Dallas, TX; *Maya
Angelou: Rainbow in the Clouds,*
WTVS-TV, Detroit, MI; and *To the
Contrary, Maryland Public Television
Tapestry and Circles*
Directed in Hollywood, 1975

Assignment America
Author of six national one half-hour
programs, interviews, and profiles,
which premiered in January, 1975

Black, Blues, Black
Ten one-hour programs on National
Education Television (NET-TV), 1968
(writer, producer and director)

*Part One: The Legacy; Part Two:
The Inheritors*
Two programs for the United States
Information Agency, 1976
(writer and host)

Touched by an Angel,
"Tree of Life" episode
1995

Runaway
CBS/Hallmark Movie,
December 10, 2000

FILMS AND PLAYS

Porgy and Bess (George Gershwin)
Played "Ruby" in European tour,
1954-55

Calypso
Off-Broadway, 1957

The Blacks (Jean Genet)
Played "White Queen" Off-Broadway,
1960; won the Obie Award in 1961

Mother Courage (Berthold Brecht)
Played starring role, Off-Broadway,
1964

Look Away (Jerome Kilty)
Played "Mrs. Keckley," Broadway, 1973

Roots (Alex Haley)
Played "Nyo Boto" (Grandmother),
1977; received an Emmy nomination for
Best Supporting Actress

How to Make an American Quilt
Universal Pictures, 1995

Down in the Delta
Miramax Films, 1998
(directorial film debut)

Madea's Family Reunion
Lion's Gate, 2006 (played the role of
"Aunt May" and read original poem,
"In and Out of Time")

RECORDINGS

Miss Calypso
Liberty Records, 1957

For the Love of Ivy
ABC Records, 1968

SPOKEN-WORD ALBUMS

The Poetry of Maya Angelou
GWP Records, 1969

Women in Business
University of Wisconsin, 1981

Been Found
Ichiban Old Indie, 1996 (music and
spoken-word album with Ashford &
Simpson)

for a few month I was a novelty
then the attendance began to wane
was told that people had come
close to listen to a real singer
riosity led me. Then came a Negro
there was a decided drop My
iveness. Night after night attenda
egan to wane until his became
mmon to find the club only a
ll at showtime I was told the
rival ____ had hired an ____
thentic singer. I went alone to
to ____ my competition and the
____ show made me come to
steps with my life.
     Della Reese was announced au
hen she ____ appeared there was an
dible gasp. She was nearly six feet
ll and very beautiful and was
aking what could be called a pro
own. There were no sequins or bea
pheny stars on her dress. She was

A Pledge to Rescue our Youth

Young women, young men of color, we add our voices to those of your ancestors who speak to you over ancient seas and across impossible mountain tops.

Come up from the gloom of national neglect. You have already been paid for.

Come out of the shadow of irrational prejudice. You owe no racial debt to history.

The blood of our bodies and the prayers of our souls have bought for you a future free from shame and bright beyond the telling of it.

We pledge ourselves and our resources to seek for you clean and well furnished schools, safe and non threatening streets, employment which makes use of your talents but does not degrade your dignity.

You are the best we have
You are all we have
You are what we have become

We pledge you our whole hearts from this day forward.

MA